INNS of the SOUTHERN MOUNTAINS

D0880592

FOR SAM

*Whose patience and sense of humor
are part of every page*

INNS of the SOUTHERN MOUNTAINS

One Hundred Scenic and Historic Hostelries
from Virginia to Georgia

Patricia L. Hudson
Photography by Sam Stapleton

EPM Publications
McLean, Virginia

Library of Congress Cataloging in Publication Data

Hudson, Patricia L.
  Inns of the Southern mountains.

   1. Hotels, taverns, etc.—Southern States—Directories.
I. Title.
TX907.H88   1985   647′.947501   84-25848
ISBN 0-914440-80-2

EPM Publications, Inc.
1003 Turkey Run Road
McLean, Virginia 22101
Printed in the United States of America

Design by Sicklesmith and Egly

Cover photograph: Fireplace at The Conyers House,
Sperryville, Virginia

CONTENTS

THE SOUTHERN MOUNTAIN STATES

NOTES
On How to Use This Guide

INNS OF THE SOUTHERN MOUNTAINS is a descriptive guide to one
hundred inns throughout the southern Appalachians, an area that includes the mountainous regions of six states: Virginia, West Virginia,
Kentucky, Tennessee, North Carolina and Georgia.

The states are covered geographically north to south, and inns are
listed alphabetically by town. The goal has been to provide the trav-
eler with a wide range of accommodations. Several criteria were used
in deciding which inns should be included. (1) The inn had to offer
overnight accommodations. "Inns" which functioned solely as restaurants were excluded. (2) The inn must, in some fashion, introduce
guests to the cultural and/or natural heritage of the southern mountains. Inns operating in historic buildings were likely candidates for
inclusion, as were those located near a site of outstanding natural
beauty.

A range of rates are quoted for each inn and are based on double
occupancy. Rates are subject to change without notice.

The author visited each of the establishments listed and the opin-
ions represented within are entirely her own. Neither free lodging
nor a fee of any sort was solicited or accepted from the innkeepers.

HEAVENLY FOOD, VIEWS AND HOSTS

"Woodpeckers—they're an innkeeper's nightmare."

"Woodpeckers?" I asked.

During months of interviewing innkeepers I'd heard stories of employee problems, broken plumbing, and off-season slumps, but this was a response I hadn't encountered.

I hurriedly scribbled "Problems—woodpecker," in my notebook as she continued.

"One woodpecker lands on the side of the inn each morning at five o'clock and begins to hammer away, waking all our guests. We've tried *everything* we can think of to scare him off."

"Hasn't anything worked?"

She sighed and shook her head. "I'm exhausted. I get up each morning before five, open an attic window, and wait for the woodpecker to land. Then I lean out the window and flap a towel like mad. That scares him away until the next morning."

I stifled a smile. "What do you do then?"

She laughed. "I go back to bed!"

After more than a year of traveling through the southern mountains staying at inns and talking with innkeepers, I'm still amazed at the pains they take to insure the comfort of their guests. The majority of innkeepers share two traits: a *genuine* concern for their guests and an unabashed affection for their mountain locale.

No matter one's interests—hiking, searching for antiques, white water rafting, or sampling the local cuisine—innkeepers are a wonderful source of information. Perhaps they know so much because they rarely miss an opportunity to learn from their guests. During interviews I frequently answered as many questions as I asked, the most common being, "Why did you decide to write about inns?"

Time after time I found myself explaining how, as a freelancer, I spent a great deal of time traveling through the southeast collecting material for magazine articles. During these trips I discovered it was far more interesting (and frequently more economical) to stay at an inn rather than one of the chain motels. No guide book existed specifically for mountain inns, so I began to compile my own listings, and the idea for the book was born.

Looking back, I realize a feeling of regional pride played a part in my pursuit of this project. As a native East Tennesseean, I'm disturbed by the clichés that cling to the region and its people. I wanted to write a book which would entice visitors off the interstates and into the mountain communities, hoping their experiences would enable them to see beyond the hillbilly stereotype.

I felt it was absolutely necessary to visit each inn, and, whenever possible, to speak with the innkeepers. To accomplish this I sandwiched "inn visits" into every available weekend, many times doing interviews for magazine assignments during the day, then returning to an inn for an evening of note-taking. During the 18 months it took to gather this material, the photographer and I drove over 9,000 miles, criss-crossing the region many times.

I endured a lot of good-natured ribbing from my friends concerning just how much "work" these trips involved, especially when I arrived home talking about the marvelous mountain scenery or a fabulous four course dinner I'd consumed, all in the line of duty.

Food is one of the best reasons to visit a mountain inn; there are endless opportunities for fine dining. Fried chicken and fresh mountain trout are still regional favorites, but one can also indulge in such dishes as veal picatta, stuffed sole, and beef Wellington. (After a few months of sampling the cuisine at inns from one end of the Appalachians to the other, I felt compelled to enroll in an exercise class.)

I returned from these trips with a much greater appreciation for the region's history, cultural vitality, and natural beauty. I learned thousands of interesting facts: that the southern mountains harbor more types of wildflowers than are found in all of Europe, that the nation's FIRST gold rush was in the Georgia mountains, that snow "falls" upward at Blowing Rock, North Carolina, and that the Barter Theatre in Abingdon, Virginia, has the nation's largest professional company in continuous residence outside New York City.

Sometimes the information I encountered concerned the supernatural rather than the factual. A great many inns claim to have ghosts in residence. The tap room of one 18th century inn is supposedly haunted by a gambler who was shot during a card game. The strains of a violin float through the halls of another inn, played, it is said, by a young woman grieving for her lover who was killed in the Civil War. At a Virginia inn a spectral woman in blue appears at a window whispering the name "Caroline."

Did I actually see any of these apparitions? No, thank goodness, but I did have one eerie experience after sitting up well past midnight to read historic documents about the inn where I was staying. The papers included several letters written by a woman who had lived in the house during the Civil War, and they were so vivid I went to bed feeling as if I'd met her.

Moments after I'd snapped off the bedside light the door to my room swung slowly, silently open. I shut my eyes in disbelief and when I opened them the door was tightly closed, just as I'd left it.

Had my eyes played tricks on me? Perhaps, but I no longer scoff quite so loudly when I'm told a ghost story.

Even without an encounter with the supernatural, visiting an inn was rarely dull. The book's photographer, Sam Stapleton, had an unexpected adventure in an antebellum inn when he wandered upstairs to take some interior shots, leaving me and the proprietor chatting in the parlor. After Sam had been gone for quite some time we began to comment on his absence and finally, to search for him.

We found him in a remote part of the house, trapped behind a locked door. The door knob had come off in his hand. He was rescued by the embarrassed innkeeper who was armed with a screwdriver and kept muttering, "I can just see what you're going to write."

If he could only know that incident has become one of my favorite memories, precisely because it is unlike any experience I might have had in the more predictable world of the modern motel. Inns offer their guests a slice of life—sometimes serene, sometimes surprising, always interesting.

Welbourne. *Middleburg, Virginia.*

VIRGINIA

Abingdon

THE MARTHA WASHINGTON INN
150 West Main Street, P.O. Box 1037
Abingdon, Virginia 24210
(703) 628-3161

The central portion of the Martha Washington was built in the early 1830s as a private residence for General Francis Preston and his wife, a niece of Patrick Henry. The stately home with its wide entrance hall, 18-foot ceilings, and tall walk-through windows, was a thank you gift from the General to his wife for bearing 15 children. On Mrs. Preston's death in 1860, the home was converted into Martha Washington College, a finishing school for young ladies of affluent families.

During the Civil War the college became a hospital, with many of the girls remaining to nurse the wounded. One young woman, known only as Beth, fell in love with an injured Yankee Captain, playing her violin to soothe him. Despite her care, the soldier died, and Beth succumbed to typhoid a short time later. For years now, visitors claim they've heard Beth's violin echoing softly through the halls at night.

Another story from the war years tells of a young soldier who slipped into the school to see his intended. Surprised by a

THE SOUTHERN MOUNTAIN STATES
(Area of map shown below)

VIRGINIA

● Abingdon

detachment of enemy soldiers, he was shot and killed on the second floor landing.

How factual are the stories? "Well," says employee Teresa Rainey, "when we restored the second floor, we uncovered the original flooring and discovered blood stains just where tradition says the soldier was killed." And what about Beth? Rainey smiles. "For generations people have insisted they've heard a violin. Recently," she laughs, "a guest who knew the stories appeared at the desk and insisted on checking out because he heard 'Beth playing.' Later, we discovered that the guest next door was listening to a concert on cable."

Martha Washington College closed its doors in the 1930s and the building was converted into an inn in 1937. The original innkeeper was an antique collector with eclectic tastes, and the inn has furnishings ranging from Renaissance to art-nouveau. "Our collection of antiques is valued at 2½ million dollars and all the pieces are in use. There are no roped off areas," says Rainey.

The inn has 70 guest rooms, all with private baths, phones and TVs. There are wood-burning fireplaces in the parlors, and a broad front porch lined with rocking chairs. The dining room, complete with white linen tablecloths and napkins, serves a variety of sandwiches for lunch and a selection of entrees, with an emphasis on steaks and seafood, for dinner.

The Barter Theatre, which sits across the street from the inn, offers excellent theatre April through mid-October. The theatre was founded during the Depression by out-of-work actors willing to perform on the barter system, charging "ham for Hamlet." Today, it is the longest running professional theatre in the country, and playgoers now use money to gain admission.

Season: Open year round.

Dining: Three meals served daily to public.

Children: Welcome.

Pets: Not permitted.

Payment: American Express, Visa, MasterCard, Carte Blanche, Diner's Club, & personal check.

Directions: Take exit eight off I-81 headed toward Abingdon. One half mile from exit, make a right turn at light onto Main Street. Inn is second building on the right.

Rates: $65, double occupancy.

Aldie

LITTLE RIVER INN
Box 116
Aldie, Virginia 22001
(703) 327-6742
Innkeepers: Tucker Withers and Monica Lee

The 20th century seems to have slipped past the tiny village of Aldie. Established in 1810 by the Virginia legislature, the town's population had grown to 100 by 1835. Today, despite the ebb and flow of many generations, Aldie still has around 100 residents.

The town grew up around a gristmill built on the banks of the Little River in 1807, and the miller, Charles Mercer, named the town in honor of his ancestral Scottish home. The old mill continued to operate until 1971, and plans are under way to restore the landmark.

During the Civil War, the Confederate Colonel, John Singleton Mosby, passed through Aldie many times leading raids against the Northern forces. Once, Mosby's men discovered several dusty Union soldiers hiding in the storage bins at the mill.

In 1982 Tucker Withers, an Aldie antique dealer, restored a two-story brick house in the center of the village. He had purchased the property several years before from the family who had owned it since 1868. Included in the deal was an eight-foot-high corner cupboard made for the family in 1810. "I opened an inn," jokes Withers, "because I wanted to have people in the house who would appreciate that piece."

At the time Withers purchased the house, the cupboard was one of its only positive features. There were 20 coats of paint on the hardwood floors, the wiring was shot, and there was no water pressure. "We had to start from scratch," says Withers.

The results of the restoration are impressive. All the furnishings date from 1800 to 1860, and Currier and Ives prints, Oriental rugs, and handmade quilts meet the eye at every turn.

There are five guest rooms in the main house (two with private baths) as well as two separate guest cottages, the Log Cabin, and the Patent House.

Withers, who serves on the Loudoun County Historic Review Committee, purchased the cabin because the previous owner planned to have it bulldozed. "The place was a mess," admits Withers, "but when we stripped off the outer layers we found solid logs."

The Patent House, which dates from the early 19th century, is only 16 x 20 feet, the minimum size necessary for a settler to qualify for a land grant. Both cottages have private baths and working fireplaces.

Season: Open year round.

Dining: No meals served to public.

Children: No young children please.

Pets: Not permitted.

Payment: Visa, MasterCard & personal check.

Directions: Thirty-five miles west of Washington, D.C. on Rt. 50 in center of Aldie.

Rates: Range from $60 to $105, double occupancy. Full breakfast included in room rate.

Banco

OLIVE MILLS
General Delivery
Banco, Virginia 22711
(703) 923-4664
Innkeeper: Phyllis Rockwell

Formerly a resident of Washington, D.C., Phyllis Rockwell moved to the country because of her fascination with old mills. "I've always loved waterwheel mills, and when I saw this one for sale I thought, 'I want it. I don't know why, but I do.'"

She moved into the mill (which had been shut down for 25 years) and began to rejuvenate it. Rockwell teaches basketry and has tried her hand at a variety of other crafts. For a while she operated a craft shop out of the mill, before deciding that retail sales took up too much time for a working craftsman.

When the two-story miller's house adjacent to the mill was put on the market, Rockwell purchased it partially for the pleasure of reuniting the properties. Then she had to decide what to do with it.

"I had enjoyed staying at bed and breakfasts when I was in Britain, and this house was certainly large enough, so I decided to try it."

Olive Mills began offering B. & B. accommodations in 1981. There are three bedrooms in the main house. The old summer kitchen behind the house can sleep four, and contains a loft/sleeping area sure to delight the young at heart. All guests share two baths located in the main house.

Rockwell has continued her work on the old mill, and the ten-foot waterwheel is functioning once again. Guests are welcome to view the ongoing work on the mill's machinery.

Season: Open year round.

Dining: No meals served to public.

Children: Welcome.

Pets: Not permitted.

Payment: No credit cards. Personal checks accepted.

Directions: On Rt. 231, five miles north of Madison in the community of Banco.

Rates: $40, double occupancy. Full breakfast included in room rate.

Charlottesville

GUESTHOUSES
P.O. Box 5737
Charlottesville, Virginia 22905
(804) 979-8327

If you've been hesitant to try the bed and breakfast experience, you will find no better introduction than Guesthouses, a reservation service that carefully matches prospective guests with accommodations in the Charlottesville area. Originated by an energetic woman named Sally Reger, Guesthouses began in 1976 and is the oldest B. & B. service in the country.

"We offer a wide variety of accommodations so our guests are able to select a situation that makes them comfortable," says Reger. Each potential listing has to pass a rigorous personal inspection by Reger. "Good B. & B. hostesses are in it primarily for the fun and that's the attitude we want our guests to encounter."

The accommodations range from rooms with the bath down the hall to cottages on country estates. "If you want privacy we'll book you into something with a private entrance, but if you want to interact with the family we can arrange that too."

Recently Reger has begun to expand the service beyond the Charlottesville area, and she now has listings in and around Luray, Virginia, a small town near the Shenandoah National Park.

Reger spends about 20 minutes on the phone with each prospective guest. "I need a good deal of information to make a good placement. We're able to offer really special accommodations because the owners know we won't send them someone with whom they'd be totally incompatible."

To make a reservation or request more information, call (804) 979-8327 or (804) 979-7264 from 1 to 6 p.m. Monday through Friday.

Churchville

BUCKHORN INN
Star Route Box 139
Churchville, Virginia 24421
(703) 885-2900
Innkeepers: Roger and Eileen Lee

In 1811, William G. Dudley, an Englishman, built a three- story house on the edge of the Virginia wilderness. In 1840 the Dudley family converted their home into a wayside inn to serve the stagecoaches journeying to the hot springs that lay to the west. Stonewall Jackson and his wife stayed at the inn in 1854, and during the Civil War it was used as a hospital.

Although the building has been in continual use as a tavern, inn or boarding house, it had become quite dilapidated. Then, in 1977, an area caterer/antique dealer restored it to use as a showcase for his business.

The present owners, Roger and Eileen Lee, are originally from New Jersey (no relation to the Lees of Virginia) and purchased the inn in 1980.

"We were very lucky," Roger says, "because we had something to build on. The previous owner stayed for a while and helped us learn the business. Even so, it took nearly a year before we felt we were getting the hang of things."

The Buckhorn has acquired a well-deserved reputation for its country cooking served buffet style. "With this type of cooking there are no exact recipes," says Lee. "You just keep working until things taste right."

The six guest rooms are upstairs, reached by a graceful staircase constructed with wooden pegs. The Stonewall Jackson Room is in the oldest portion of the inn and has a private bath, while the other five rooms and two shared baths are in a wing which was added in 1929. Decorated in American country style, the rooms have televisions, but no phones.

One senses the inn's pioneer past most strongly downstairs in the old tavern room with its large fireplace and wide pine paneling that has been laboriously cleaned of decades of paint. Still in use as a dining area, the room seems to echo with the laughter of the mountain men who once frequented it.

Season: Open year round.

Dining: Lunch and dinner served to public. Restaurant closed on Mondays.

Children: Welcome.

Pets: Discouraged.

Payment: Visa, MasterCard & personal check.

Directions: Take exit 57 off I-81. Follow Rt. 250 west through Staunton and Churchville. Inn is on right approximately 18 miles off interstate.

Rates: Range from $28 to $38, double occupancy. Continental breakfast included in room rate, but full breakfast available for guests on request.

Hot Springs

THE HOMESTEAD
Hot Springs, Virginia 24445
(703) 839-5500

The 104 degree water at Hot Springs has been drawing a crowd since colonial days. In 1750 Dr. Thomas Walker, a medical missionary traveling through the mountains, wrote, "We went to Hot Springs and found six invalids there. The spring is very clear and warmer than new milk. . . ."

The first inn was built in 1766 by Thomas Bullitt because his home was perpetually overrun with uninvited guests. Today, the springs still attract a crowd, but The Homestead is prepared to handle them.

The Homestead's size is staggering; it contains more than six hundred guest rooms and can entertain over 1,000 guests. The original Homestead burned in 1901, and the present structure, with frequent additions over the years, dates from 1902.

The spa facilities are still a major attraction, and hydrotherapy is offered under medical supervision. In addition the resort offers an astonishing variety of activities; everything from skiing to golf to carriage rides.

Over the years The Homestead has hosted many famous guests including Woodrow Wilson, Lyndon Johnson, and the Eisenhowers.

Season: Open year round.

Dining: All three meals served daily to public.

Children: Welcome.

Pets: Phone inn for current policy.

Payment: American Express, Visa, MasterCard & personal check.

Directions: On U.S. 220 in Hot Springs.

Rates: Range from $196 to $310, double occupancy. Breakfast and dinner included in room rate (Modified American Plan).

VINE COTTAGE INN
P. O. Box 205
Hot Springs, Virginia 24445
(703) 839-2422
Innkeeper: Doug O'Brien

Vine Cottage offers a nice change of pace in an area where large resorts are the rule. It is just steps away from the Homestead with its countless recreational facilities, but provides guests with a homelike atmosphere.

Owner Doug O'Brien also runs Sam Snead's Tavern, one of the favorite dining spots in Hot Springs, and guests at the cottage usually wend their way down the street to sample the fare. Vine Cottage was built in 1901, probably as an annex for the Homestead. In the 1930s the inn and its proprietor, "Miss Sallie," were quite famous for hospitality and homestyle cooking.

Today, the inn's 16 rooms are decorated in country style; and a variety of accommodations, from single rooms to suites, are available.

Season: Open year round, except the first two weeks of December.
Dining: No meals served to public.
Children: Welcome.
Pets: Permitted, if "small and well-behaved".
Payment: Visa, MasterCard & personal check.
Directions: On Route 220, just before the entrance to the Homestead.
Rates: Range from $40 to $80, double occupancy. Continental breakfast included in room rate.

Leesburg

LAUREL BRIGADE
20 W. Market Street
Leesburg, Virginia 22075
(703) 777-1010
Innkeeper: Ellen Wall

There has been an inn on Leesburg's lot No. 30 since 1759. The present stone building was constructed in 1820, with a wing added in 1825 for the express purpose (according to local tradition) of entertaining the Marquis de Lafayette when he visited James Monroe at his home nearby.

The inn was converted to a private residence in 1854 by a local physician, Dr. A.R. Mott, and many of the building's finest features (Swiss doors, French marble mantels) were added at that time.

In 1945 Ray Flippo purchased the property at public auction and converted the old stone structure back to its original purpose, opening the Laurel Brigade in 1949.

The inn is now run by Flippo's daughter, Ellen Wall. "My father was a pioneer in a sense," says Wall. "In the early 50s the trend was toward motels. Inns were old fashioned, but father had a lot of wisdom. We're still here—many motels are not."

Six rooms are available, all with private baths, and are decorated with a variety of antiques and reproductions. There are no televisions or phones. The inn's dining room is a favorite with area residents as well as guests, and features such southern dishes as fried chicken and apple pie. All pastries and breads are homemade.

The name, Laurel Brigade, is in honor of a Confederate cavalry brigade which fought at Appomattox and refused to surrender. The brigade's leader removed his men from the field and rode off to Lynchburg where the group quietly disbanded.

The inn is located in "downtown" Leesburg, a small Virginia town with interesting architecture and a well-prepared walking tour to help you enjoy the sights. Visitors should stop by the Museum and Visitor's Center (16 West Loudoun Street) where information and a 15-minute slide orientation are available.

Season: Open year round except January 1 through February 15.
Dining: Lunch and dinner served to public. Restaurant closed on Monday.
Children: Welcome.
Pets: Permitted.
Payment: No credit cards. Personal checks accepted.
Directions: One half block west of the junction of Rt. 15 and Rt. 7 in Leesburg.
Rates: Range from $32 to $53, double occupancy.

NORRIS HOUSE INN
108 West Loudoun Street, S.W.
Leesburg, Virginia 22075
(703) 777-1806
Innkeepers: Amy and Craig DeRemer

Located in Leesburg's historic district, the Norris House is a bed and breakfast inn run by a young couple with a real sense of Virginia hospitality. The house was built in 1806, and the DeRemers purchased it in 1983 from the Norris family who had owned it for more than 100 years.

The DeRemers had planned to open an inn "years in the future—when we retired." But a weekend excursion found them in Leesburg and they fell in love with its small town atmosphere.

"The inn is not extraordinarily profitable," says Amy, "but you do get to live as if you have money—surrounded by beautiful things." The DeRemers supplement their income with other endeavors including a management service for inns and other small businesses.

There are four guest rooms (two shared baths) and two of the rooms have working fireplaces. Antiques fill the place; about half are family pieces, such as the quilts used as wall hangings that once belonged to Amy's grandmother.

Guests are pampered with extra touches such as handmade

chocolates on their pillows, port and sherry served in the evening, and packets of bubble bath invitingly displayed in the baths. The inn's full breakfast features fresh juice, home brewed coffee, and a different main dish each morning. Salmon quiche is a favorite.
Season: Open year round.
Dining: No meals served to public.
Children: No young children, please.
Pets: Not permitted.
Payment: No credit cards. Personal checks accepted.
Directions: Located in the historic district, one block from the Visitor's Center.
Rates: Range from $55 to $85, double occupancy. Full breakfast included in room rate.

Lexington

HISTORIC COUNTRY INNS OF LEXINGTON
11 North Main Street
Lexington, Virginia 24450
(703) 463-2044
Innkeeper: Don Fredenburg

Lexington is a college town, home to both Virginia Military Institute (VMI) and Washington and Lee University. Because the community has made a conscious effort to preserve its heritage, a stroll down Lexington's streets is a walk into the past.

Two historic buildings, situated across from each other on Main Street, have been converted into overnight accommodations. Built in 1789, the Alexander-Withrow house was restored in 1972 and has six suites, each furnished with antiques and equipped with private bath, phone, refrigerator and TV (discreetly hidden in the closet). The building's exterior brick work is particularly interesting.

The McCampbell Inn, built in 1809 and restored in 1982, has 14 rooms and two suites, all furnished in the same manner as those in the Withrow. Guests are served a continental breakfast, featuring homemade muffins, in the dining area of the McCampbell Inn. No other meals are served, but there are several restaurants within walking distance. The office for the two inns is located in the McCampbell, and all guests should check in there.

After the Civil War, General Robert E. Lee accepted the presidency of tiny Washington College, and his brief tenure saw the institution gain a national reputation as a liberal arts school for men. The Lee Chapel, on the college campus, was designed by the General and possesses a simple but striking interior. Lee's basement office is just as he left it on the day of his death.

Other noteworthy sites include the Stonewall Jackson home, the VMI Museum, and the George C. Marshall Museum. The Historic Lexington Visitor Center, located at 107 East Washington Street, offers an audio-visual program and self-guided walking tour.

Season: Open year round.

Dining: No meals served to public.

Children: Welcome.

Pets: Not permitted, but arrangements for kenneling may be made in advance.

Payment: Visa, MasterCard & personal check.

Directions: Both inns are on Main Street in downtown Lexington.

Rates: Range from $47 to $62, double occupancy. Continental breakfast included in room rate.

Middleburg

RED FOX TAVERN & STRAY FOX INN
Box 385
Middleburg, Virginia 22117
(703) 687-6301
Innkeepers: Turner and Dana Reuter, Jr.

The Red Fox has been known by many names over the years, but the tavern has dispensed hearty Virginia hospitality to travelers for over 250 years. The tavern's long and illustrious history began in 1728 when Joseph Chinn opened an ordinary on the coach road which ran between Alexandria and Winchester.

By 1812 the inn was well established, possessing 35 rooms and an extensive wine cellar. In the years preceding the Revolution, its 30-inch stone walls harbored British soldiers as well as rebellious colonists.

During the Civil War, wounded Confederate troops filled the tavern's public rooms while Jeb Stuart and Colonel Mosby held meetings upstairs. The bar still in use in the Tap Room is made from one of the field operating tables used by the surgeon who ministered to Stuart's troops.

In this century, the inn has hosted many famous guests, including John F. Kennedy, who chose the pine-paneled Jeb Stuart room as the site of one of his press conferences.

The inn's 18th century atmosphere is enhanced by documented wallpapers, fabrics and paint colors of the period. Seven dining rooms, two on the ground floor and five upstairs, offer fine dining in an elegant atmosphere. Polished pine floors are accented with braided rugs, and the four guest rooms located in the Red Fox have canopied beds, private baths and working fireplaces.

Just up the street is the Stray Fox Inn, a recently restored antebellum home containing eight additional guest rooms, all with private baths and most with working fireplaces.

Season: Open year round.

Dining: Three meals served daily to public. Reservations suggested.

Children: Welcome.

Pets: Not permitted, but arrangements for kenneling may be made in advance.

Payment: American Express, Visa, MasterCard & personal check.

Directions: Located on the north side of Rt. 50 in the heart of Middleburg.

Rates: Range from $65 to $175, double occupancy.

WELBOURNE
Middleburg, Virginia 22117
(703) 687-3201
Innkeeper: Mrs. N.H. Morison

When you push open Welbourne's heavy front door and step inside, the boundaries between the past and present begin to blur. Oil portraits in heavy gilt frames, worn Oriental rugs, and antiques of every imaginable kind speak of a home which has sheltered the same family since 1820.

The central portion of the house was constructed in 1820 by adding on to a small stone house built in 1775. (The 18th century structure is the dining/kitchen area of the present house.)

"When I was a boy my grandmother showed me that the kitchen door was made so a bar could be thrown across it, supposedly to guard against Indian attacks," says Nat Morison, the sixth generation of his family to call Welbourne home. One of Nat's forefathers was a friend of George Washington, and his great-great grandfather, Richard Henry Dulany, was a Colonel in the Confederate cavalry.

"The War" left the house intact, but family letters describe the constant presence of troops and the destruction of the estate's barns and crops. The Colonel's twelve-year-old daughter wrote in her journal, "The Bible says love your enemies—but I do not believe it ever meant the Yankees."

When one lives so closely with the past, memories fade very slowly. "Once my great-grandmother asked the local car dealer to bring several cars out for her to look over, and the fellow brought a Lincoln. BIG mistake," grins Nat.

The home's recent history is equally interesting. Editor Maxwell Perkins was a family friend and occasionally brought a famous client such as Thomas Wolfe or F. Scott Fitzgerald to Welbourne for a holiday.

There are seven guest rooms (all with private baths) and three cottages. The rooms are fitted with antiques accumulated over the years, and several rooms have working fireplaces. Mrs. Morison is a gracious hostess who presides over breakfast, pouring the coffee and encouraging guests to eat hearty helpings of such southern favorites as grits and fried apples.

Season: Open year round.

Dining: No meals served to public.

Children: Welcome.

Pets: Permitted.

Payment: American Express & personal check.

Directions: Take Rt. 50 out of Middleburg going west. After 3.5 miles turn right on Rt. 611, go 1.5 miles, turn left on Rt. 743. Road will turn to dirt. Continue for 1.2 miles. Driveway is on left.

Rates: Range from $80 to $90, double occupancy. Full breakfast included in room rate.

Middletown

WAYSIDE INN SINCE 1797
7783 Main Street
Middletown, Virginia 22645
(703) 869-1797
Innkeeper: Charles Alverson

The Wayside Inn has operated continuously since 1797 with only a brief disruption during the Civil War. The original two-story building served as a stagecoach stop for travelers in the Shenandoah Valley, and wings were added in 1908 to accommodate the ever increasing traffic. As the inn expanded in the 19th century, it grew over and around a brick slave kitchen which was rediscovered in the 1960s when the inn was renovated. Dating back to the 1740s, the kitchen is now a dining area with a low-beamed ceiling, an oversized fireplace and loads of atmosphere.

The inn's owner, Leo Bernstein, a Washington banker and enthusiastic collector of antiques, has filled the inn with 18th century pieces. "We don't bother with reproductions because they don't stand up to regular use," says Chuck Alverson, the inn's general manager and a former employee of Colonial Williamsburg. "Antiques are really a better value; they were made to be lived on and around."

The inn has seven dining rooms and 21 guest rooms, all with private baths. None of the rooms has television, and only a few have phones. Each is decorated differently, but all have a colonial motif.

The dining room, where the waiters and waitresses are in colonial garb, offers a variety of food, including several selections that reflect the region's culinary heritage. Along with the traditional prime rib or fried chicken, one can order rabbit, or a huntsman's pie which contains venison, duck and rabbit in a port-wine sauce. "It took us about six months of diligent searching to locate a source for venison, but we finally did it," says Alverson.

Season: Open year round.
Dining: Three meals served daily to public.
Children: Welcome.
Pets: Not permitted.
Payment: American Express, Visa, MasterCard, Diner's Club, Carte Blanche & personal check.

Directions: Take exit 77 off I-81. Follow Rt. 11 into town.
Rates: Range from $55 to $95, double occupancy.

Monterey

HIGHLAND INN
Main Street, P.O. Box 40
Monterey, Virginia 24465
(703) 468-2143
Innkeepers: George Saunders and Robert Campbell

Built in 1904, the Highland was vacant when George Saunders
purchased it in 1981. Now, lots of hard work and half a million dollars
later, the inn has been restored to its original turn of the century
style and is listed on the National Register.

The inn has 20 guest rooms, all with private baths, and boasts an
excellent dining room where the house specialty is fresh trout,
cooked to order.

"The Highland was once known as 'The Pride of the Mountains'"
says George Saunders, "but its reputation had deteriorated as badly
as the building. We've worked hard to re-establish quality service for
our guests."

The town of Monterey, population 379, doesn't possess a single
traffic light. Known for its maple sugar, the town hosts a Maple
Festival each March which features demonstrations of syrup making.

Three and a half million acres of National Forest surround the
town, and the inn's mountain setting is practical as well as beautiful.
"The building doesn't have air-conditioning," says Saunders. "We just
don't need it because the temperature remains pleasant all summer."
Season: Open all year.
Dining: Three meals served daily to public.
Children: Welcome.
Pets: Permitted.
Payment: American Express, Visa, MasterCard, Diner's Club, Carte
Blanche & personal check.
Directions: Located just off Rt. 220 in "downtown" Monterey.
Rates: Range from $38 to $72, double occupancy.

Mayhurst Inn. *Orange, Virginia.*

Orange

MAYHURST INN
P.O. Box 707
Orange, Virginia 22960
(804) 293-6382, or (703) 672-5597
Innkeepers: Stephen and Shirley Ramsey

On first sight, Mayhurst looks like a frothy dollop of whipped cream balanced on a green Virginia hilltop. From its arched windows to the ornate belvedere high atop the house, Mayhurst's architectural exuberance is a source of amazement for all who view it.

Colonel John Willis, a prominent landowner and grandnephew of James Madison, built the house in 1859. The home became the headquarters for the Army of Northern Virginia during the winter of 1863-64, and Stonewall Jackson is said to have surveyed troop movements from the belvedere which offers a fine view of the countryside.

Stephen and Shirley Ramsey, who formerly operated the Crossroads Inn at North Garden, Virginia, purchased Mayhurst with an eye toward expanding their bed and breakfast business. "We had a very limited number of guest rooms at North Garden, and when we happened upon Mayhurst we just fell for it," says Shirley.

Although the home stood empty for several years prior to the Ramseys' purchase, it is in surprisingly good condition. A graceful spiral staircase connects the four floors. The inn has seven guest rooms, all with private baths and many with fireplaces. Although they may add a few more rooms, the Ramseys plan to stay small. Says Shirley, "Inns turn into something else if they get too big."

The Ramseys also run an antique business (which will eventually be housed in a barn at the rear of the house) and the inn is slowly filling with antiques. "We're really just getting started," Shirley explains. "We brought most of the furniture that's here from North Garden, and there just wasn't enough to fill a house this size."
Season: Open year round.
Dining: No meals served to public.
Children: Welcome.
Pets: Permitted, with prior approval.

Payment: No credit cards. Personal checks accepted.
Directions: In Orange, follow Rt. 15 south. Just out of town, watch for grassy median. Once it begins, take first driveway on the right.
Rates: Range from $47 to $75, double occupancy. Full breakfast and afternoon tea included in room rate.

Sperryville

THE CONYERS HOUSE
Slate Mills Road
Sperryville, Virginia 22740
(703) 987-8025
Innkeepers: Sandra and Norman Cartwright-Brown

The Conyers House is a country inn with more than a dash of city sophistication. Innkeeper Sandra Cartwright-Brown, formerly of Washington D.C., has boundless energy. She is an avid antique collector, active in the Washington social scene, travels extensively (she and husband Norman speak French, German, Italian, and a smattering of Arabic) and has recently added innkeeping to her accomplishments.

When the Cartwright-Browns purchased a rundown farm house in 1979, their plans were to create a private country retreat. But when an extended business trip took Norman out of the country, Sandra hit upon the idea of a bed and breakfast inn and proceeded full steam ahead. Plans for the inn were well under way upon Norman's return.

The oldest portion of The Conyers House dates back to 1770 and was in use as a general store by the early 1800s. During the restoration Sandra discovered some store accounts penciled onto a door frame, including a reminder to "Put hogs in pen to fatten," dated October 14, 1864. The old store room is now the living area, with a grand piano in one corner, floor to ceiling bookshelves, and numerous Chinese rugs.

Antiques, gathered from such far flung places as Munich and New Brunswick, fill the house, and many of them have entertaining stories which Sandra, who has a real comic flair, will relate on request.

A new three-story wing was added in 1979 and was the first portion of the house to have central heating. Up to that time the

The Conyers House. *Sperryville, Virginia.*

numerous fireplaces were the only source of heat. Certain areas of the house still depend on wood heat, supplemented by electric heaters. "In winter our guests understand why their forefathers wore flannel to bed," says Sandra.

There are six guest rooms, two with private baths, as well as two cottages: the Hill House, which is 30 paces from the main house, and the Spring House, which was once used to cool dairy products.

Breakfast is served in "sittings." Guests simply sign up on a list posted on the refrigerator. The meal is a feast for the eye as well as the palate, with red pepper jelly, English muffins slathered in cream cheese, farm fresh sausage, cheese strata, applesauce cake, and REAL cream supplied by a neighboring farmer. Other meals may be arranged if plenty of advance notice is given. In addition, The Inn at Little Washington, considered one of the finest French restaurants on the east coast, is only 15 minutes away.

Since her move to the country, Sandra has become an avid equestrian, riding to the hounds with the Rappahannock Hunt, an activity she will gladly share with interested guests. There are plenty of hiking trails nearby, as well as tubing in the Hughes River, "but only," says Sandra "if the local church isn't baptizing."

Season: Open year round.
Dining: Dinner served to guests and public if reservations are made well in advance.
Children: No small children, please.
Pets: By prior arrangement only.
Payment: No credit cards. Personal checks accepted.
Directions: Turn left off Rt. 211 at Sperryville Emporium, then left at blinking light onto Rt. 522. Follow 522 ¾ of a mile and turn right onto Rt. 231. Go eight miles and turn left onto Rt. 707. Proceed .6 of a mile. Inn is on left.
Rates: Range from $70 to $100, double occupancy. Full breakfast and afternoon tea included in room rate.

NETHER'S MILL
Rt. 1, Box 62
Sperryville, Virginia 22740
(703) 987-8625
Innkeeper: Worden Robinson

Worden Robinson is a man of many talents who has taken 20 acres
along the Hughes River and launched not only a bed and breakfast,
but several other ventures as well. The old mill, its grinding stones
intact, houses a craft shop featuring Robinson's pottery. Another
outbuilding contains a workshop where he manufactures pottery
kilns, and the mill race has been dammed to form a trout pond. For a
small fee, you can try your hand at fishing. (Nethers Mill trout are
delivered weekly to many of the area's best restaurants.) In addition,
Robinson raises a small number of hogs and produces gourmet
sausage, hams and soap.

The two guest rooms are on the second floor of the turn of the
century miller's house. To reach them one passes through a screened
porch filled with tools (this is after all a WORKING farm) and up a
narrow stairway, to rooms that are clean and comfortably furnished.

"I get mainly the outdoor types," Robinson explains. "This place
wouldn't appeal to people who are used to posh." The house sits at
the foot of Old Rag Mountain (elevation 3,291) and is a good base of
operations for hiking and other outdoor activities. The Hughes River,
which flows beside the house, contains bass and trout, as well as an
occasional canoeist.

An old wood stove dominates the kitchen, and Robinson cooks
guests a hearty breakfast that includes fresh rainbow trout and
homemade bread. After a hard day's work on the farm, Robinson
enjoys lounging in the kitchen talking to guests. "There's nothing
much to do out here after dark except relax," he says.

Season: Open year round.
Dining: No meals served to public.
Children: Welcome.
Pets: Permitted.
Payment: No credit cards. Personal checks accepted.
Directions: On Rt. 211, turn left at Sperryville Emporium and left
again at the light onto Rt. 522. Go ¾ of a mile and turn right onto Rt.
231. Stay on Rt. 231 for eight miles following Old Rag Mountain
signs, and take a right onto Rt. 601. Take another right at bottom of

hill and go 2.8 miles. Mill will be on your right.
Rates: $50, double occupancy. Full breakfast included in room rate.

Stanley

JORDAN HOLLOW FARM INN
Rt. 2, Box 375
Stanley, Virginia 22851
(703) 778-2209 and 778-2285
Innkeepers: Marley and Jetze Beers

Marley and Jetze Beers have taken a 200-year-old horse farm and
turned it into a country retreat where the horse is king. "About 50%
of our guests choose our inn because of our emphasis on equestrian
activities," explains Jetze.

The Beers' have 19 horses and, for a nominal stabling charge,
guests may bring their own mounts along on vacation. Trail riding
near the Shenandoah National Park is a favorite pastime, and riding
lessons are available as Marley is an "A" rated instructor with years
of experience teaching, training and showing.

Jordan Hollow also offers swimming, hiking and plain old porch
sitting. "We're a non-pretentious type of place," says Jetze, a tall
Dutchman with a friendly smile. "We're doing everything possible to
keep the inn low key."

Despite its remote country setting the inn has an international
flavor. Marley's collection of African carvings (a souvenir of her days
in the Peace Corps) are mixed in with antiques, artwork and crafts
from around the world. Meals are "country cosmopolitan"—a little bit
like Grandma's and a little bit French, with traces of African and mid-
eastern seasonings.

A 19th century farm house with two 18th century log cabins at its
core serves as the Beers' home and also houses the dining areas.
"We had no idea the log structures were there until we started the
renovation," says Marley. Today, the original log walls are visible in
several of the dining rooms.

Twenty guest rooms, all with private baths, are located in a just-
completed lodge set alongside the farm house. The rooms are
decorated with country furnishings that create a cozy feeling.
Season: Open year round.

Dining: All three meals served to public, by reservation only.
Children: Welcome.
Pets: Horses boarded. Dogs and cats not permitted at inn, but
kenneling is available nearby.
Payment: Visa, MasterCard & personal check.
Directions: Follow Rt. 689 out of Stanley to Rt. 626. Turn right and go
1.6 miles to farm driveway on right.
Rates: Range from $36 to $53, double occupancy. Room rate includes
three meals, served family-style.

Strasburg

HOTEL STRASBURG
201 Holliday Street
Strasburg, Virginia 22657
(703) 465-9191
Innkeeper: Michael Paper

This three-story Victorian hotel sits on a quiet corner in downtown
Strasburg, population 2,400. The building was built in the 1860s as a
hospital and was later converted into a rooming house. In the
mid-70s a complete restoration was undertaken which transformed
the building into a hotel that showcases Victorian furnishings.

There are 17 guest rooms on the upper floors; only some have
private baths, but remodeling plans call for additional baths to be
added in the near future. The rooms are outfitted with antiques and
all the furnishings are for sale. Innkeeper Michael Paper is also
involved with the Strasburg Emporium, a large antique warehouse
whose ample stock supplies the hotel with period pieces. "I like to
redecorate," says Paper, "so if a guest likes something I'm usually
willing to sell it to make room for something else."

Paper is quick to point out that the hotel's dining room is its
biggest drawing card. "We specialize in GOOD food. You can't really
classify it—we cook all sorts of dishes." Everything is homemade,
right down to the salad dressings. The soups are especially good, and
one self-proclaimed chili connoisseur declares that the Strasburg's
chili is "the best anywhere."
Season: Open all year.
Dining: Breakfast, lunch and dinner served daily to public.

Children: Welcome.

Pets: Not permitted.

Payment: American Express, Visa, MasterCard, & personal check.

Directions: Take exit 75 off I-81 onto Rt. 11 South and follow it to Rt. 55. Upon entering Strasburg, take right at first light and a left at the next light. Hotel is down one block on the left.

Rates: Range from $35 to $60, double occupancy.

Trevilians

PROSPECT HILL
Trevilians, Virginia 23170
(703) 967-0844
Innkeepers: Mireille and Bill Sheehan

Prospect Hill is tucked away in a grove of trees in the rolling countryside just east of Charlottesville. Hidden in the center of the rambling white frame house is a log barn built in 1732. "The family who settled here lost their cabin in a fire," explains Melvin Henson, the inn's jovial manager, "so they moved into the barn and over the years this house grew up around it."

During the latter part of the 18th century sturdy brick slave quarters were built on the property, and in 1840 a wealthy landowner, William Overton, purchased the farm and enlarged the house by adding a spiral staircase and two wings. Financially ruined by the Civil War, the Overtons began taking in guests, and in the 1880s a final addition to the house was made.

The Sheehans purchased the old Overton home in 1977, and filled the inn with their family antiques. There are seven guest rooms, all with private baths, and six with working fireplaces. "We'll get the fire STARTED for you," says Henson, "and after that we just point you in the direction of the woodshed." Several of the guest rooms are in the restored slave quarters which stand alongside the main house.

Forty acres of farm land surround the inn, a remnant of the once grand plantation that covered more than 1,500 acres and produced quantities of wheat and corn. Large boxwoods, some nearly 200 years old, line the front walk.

Guests are served a full breakfast, and may dine in their room if they desire. Dinner is served in the candlelit dining room and there is no menu. All the cooking is done by Bill Sheehan, who prepares a four- or five-course meal which varies according to his mood. The dishes show a strong French influence (Mireille is French) and guests seem quite content to consume whatever is served.

Season: Open year round.

Dining: Dinner served to public, Wednesday through Saturday, by reservation only.

Children: Welcome, but no facilities for infants.

Pets: Not permitted.

Payment: Visa, MasterCard & personal check.

Directions: On I-64, take exit 27 onto Rt. 15 south. Turn left on Rt. 250 east at Zion's Crossroads. Go one mile to Rt. 613, turn left and go three miles.

Rates: Range from $80 to $100, double occupancy. Full breakfast included in room rate.

Vesuvius

SUGAR TREE LODGE
Rt. 56
Vesuvius, Virginia 24483
(703) 377-2197
Innkeepers: Richard Meeth and Dean Gregory

Nestled in the woods on a steep mountain slope, Sugar Tree Lodge is just one and a quarter miles off the Blue Ridge Parkway. The lodge is constructed of handhewn oak, chestnut and poplar logs from six pioneer structures.

Dr. Richard Meeth, a Washington educational consultant, built the lodge over a period of five years intending to make it his private retreat, a fact which accounts for the inn's undeniably homey atmosphere.

There are now three buildings on the property (the Lodge, Guesthouse and Gatehouse) with a total of eight guest rooms, all with private baths and antique furnishings. Most of the rooms have working fireplaces as well. "We want to remain a quiet, quaint inn, so we don't plan to expand beyond 14 rooms," says Dean Gregory, the resident manager.

The Lodge consists of a great room, library, three guest rooms, and the dining areas. Upon entering the great room, one's eye is drawn to the massive limestone fireplace that dominates the lodge interior. The two dining rooms, one a glass addition that opens off the great room, can seat up to 40 diners.

Sugar Tree is developing a well-deserved reputation for high quality continental cuisine. "Our goal," says Gregory, "is to win a four star rating from the Mobile guide—which is a lot to expect from a relatively new establishment."

The menu ranges from fresh trout to veal picatta, and all dishes have been thoroughly tested before being offered to the public. Says Gregory, "We're striving for consistency. EVERY dish has to be good." Even the crackers are homemade, and the desserts are a special treat, particularly the house specialty, chocolate whiskey pie.

Gregory, who pinch hits in the kitchen and occasionally waits tables, has an eye for detail that accounts for several decorative surprises. Instead of the usual silver, the tableware is gold. "I saw it used in a San Francisco restaurant and thought it gave the table a special look," says Gregory. "It certainly generates a lot of comments."

Season: Open early April to early December.

Dining: Lunch and dinner served to public by reservation.

Children: Discouraged.

Pets: Allowed in Gatehouse accommodations only.

Payment: Visa, MasterCard & personal check.

Directions: From I-81, take exit 54 and turn east on Rt. 606. Go 1½ miles to U.S. 11 and turn left. Go 50 yards and turn right on Rt. 56. Go four miles (through Vesuvius) to Lodge.

Rates: $60, double occupancy. Full breakfast included in room rate.

The Inn at Gristmill Square. *Warm Springs, Virginia.*

Warm Springs

THE INN AT GRISTMILL SQUARE
P.O. Box 359
Warm Springs, Virginia 24484
(703) 839-2231
Innkeepers: Janice and Jack McWilliams

Gristmill Square, located in the village of Warm Springs, is a collection of restored 19th century shops, including the inn, a country store, art gallery and the Waterwheel restaurant. The building that houses the restaurant was once a gristmill, and although the present building only dates back to 1900, there has been a mill on the site since 1771. The Waterwheel's gourmet fare has made it justifiably famous.

The complex, with its tasteful color schemes, immaculate surroundings, quality food and accommodations, may remind the visitor of a miniature Williamsburg.

Janice and Jack McWilliams, formerly innkeepers in Vermont, purchased the property in 1981. Their move south was prompted, says Jack, "by a search for warmer weather."

The inn offers a variety of accommodations at a variety of prices, and every room is decorated differently, some with antiques, others in contemporary style. Tennis courts and a swimming pool are located on the grounds.

Season: Open year round except for first two weeks of March.
Dining: Lunch served May 1 through November 1. Dinner served year round except on Sunday when only buffet lunch is served. Restaurant closed on Monday.
Children: Welcome.
Pets: Permitted.
Payment: American Express, Visa, MasterCard & personal check.
Directions: Located in the middle of Warm Springs.
Rates: Range from $60 to $90, double occupancy. Continental breakfast included in room rate.

MEADOW LANE LODGE
Star Route A, Box 110
Warm Springs, Virginia 24484
(703) 839-5959
Innkeepers: Philip and Catherine Hirsh

Meadow Lane's 1,600 acres have long been a working farm. An old slave cabin stands near the site of an 18th century plantation house, and an overgrown race track speaks of the day when the farm was used to raise and train Thoroughbred horses. The present owner, Philip Hirsh, a native of Warm Springs, has transformed the acreage into a working cattle farm and country getaway, with tennis, swimming, hiking and fishing on the premises.

The rambling farm house that serves as the guest lodge sits in the midst of well-tended pastures. Meadow Lane accepts only 16 guests at a time, and these fortunate few are given the run of the farm. A scenic two-mile stretch of the Jackson River, well stocked with trout, flows through the estate, and the site of Fort Dinwiddie, an early colonial outpost against Indian uprisings, is on the grounds.

Hirsh has a penchant for restoring things. He was the original owner of the Inn at Gristmill Square before selling it to concentrate on Meadow Lane. Francisco Cottage, an 1820 hand-hewn cabin in Warm Springs' historic district, was a third restoration project. Hirsh discovered the cabin in the midst of a ramshackle Victorian house. The larger building was stripped away, revealing the pioneer structure. The cottage, now available for guests, is Mr. Hirsh's special pride.

Season: Open April 1 through January 31.
Dining: No meals served to public.
Children: Only with prior approval.
Pets: Only with prior approval.
Payment: American Express, Visa, MasterCard & personal check.
Directions: Follow Route 39 to Lodge entrance, four miles west of Warm Springs.
Rates: Range from $67 to $90, double occupancy. Full breakfast included in room rate.

Wintergreen

TRILLIUM HOUSE
Box 280
Wintergreen, Virginia 22958
(804) 325-9126
Innkeepers: Betty and Ed Dinwiddie

Wintergreen is a 10,000-acre resort community just a stone's throw from the Blue Ridge Parkway. In the past, visitors to Wintergreen rented a house or condominium, which provided a rather impersonal introduction to this massive complex. Betty and Ed Dinwiddie decided the resort needed a taste of country hospitality, and Trillium House is the result.

A 12-room inn set on the resort's 17th fairway, Trillium House was designed by the Dinwiddies to provide guests with modern amenities in a personalized setting. "We are not actually a part of Wintergreen," Ed explains. "We are leasing the land with an option to buy, but our guests have all the privileges of resort guests."

All manner of recreational facilities are available, from skiing to horseback riding. Over half of the acreage has been set aside as a nature preserve, and hiking trails abound.

The inn, a brand-new structure built in 1983, includes such old-fashioned touches as dormer windows, ceiling fans, and a woodstove. Each room has a private bath, and all are furnished with Dinwiddie family pieces. In addition, each room has individual heat and air as well as double-thick walls to ensure privacy.

Guests are served a buffet breakfast every morning except Sunday, when a continental breakfast is available. The inn's dining room can seat 60, and buffet dinners are served by reservation. "It's as easy to cook for 40 as it is for four," says Betty, who handles the kitchen.

Season: Open year round.
Dining: Dinner served to public by reservation.
Children: By prior arrangement only.
Pets: By prior arrangement only.
Payment: Visa, MasterCard & personal check.
Directions: On Rt. 151, follow signs to Wintergreen Mountain Resort. Stop at gate to check in. Continue 2½ miles to top of mountain.
Rates: $80, double occupancy. Full breakfast included in room rate (Continental on Sunday.)

The Country Inn. *Berkeley Springs, West Virginia.*

WEST VIRGINIA

Berkeley Springs

THE COUNTRY INN
Berkeley Springs, West Virginia 25411
(304) 258-2210
Innkeepers: Jack and Adele Barker

The Country Inn stands beside the warm springs that have made this small town a resort since the country's earliest days. George Washington was a regular visitor to the springs, having first encountered them as a teenager while surveying Lord Fairfax's western lands. In 1776 Fairfax conveyed the springs and 50 acres to the colony of Virginia, and bath houses were constructed.

In the early 1970s, the Barkers arrived in Berkeley Springs so that Adele, who had been injured in a fall, could undergo water therapy. The Barkers stayed at the inn for three months and enjoyed it so much they wound up buying it.

The inn blends the best of the past with the present. Although it has expanded over the years (it now has over 70 guest rooms), it has retained the warm feeling of a much smaller establishment. Most of the rooms have private baths, with only a few having shared facilities.

Everything, from guest rooms to the dining area, is absolutely

THE SOUTHERN MOUNTAIN STATES
(Area of map shown below)

Berkeley
Springs

Harpers
Ferry

WEST VIRGINIA

Lewisburg
White Sulphur
Springs

spotless. William North, the inn's general manager, has an eagle eye when it comes to dust. Says North, "There's nothing charming about an old inn that's dirty."

Each room is decorated in a comfortable, country style, and all have TVs. "When I first bought the inn," Jack Barker recalls, "I said I wouldn't have TVs in the rooms, but guests kept checking out because they couldn't watch their soap operas."

The inn has two dining areas, a wood-paneled room in colonial style, and an indoor country garden with skylights and hundreds of live plants. The menu offers something for everyone. All pies and breads are homemade, and the house specialty is fried fruit fritters.

Season: Open year round.
Dining: Three meals are served daily to public.
Children: Welcome.
Pets: Not permitted, but arrangements for kenneling may be made in advance.
Payment: American Express, Visa, MasterCard & personal check.
Directions: Adjacent to Berkeley Springs State Park in the town of Berkeley Springs.
Rates: Range from $35 to $50, double occupancy.

Harpers Ferry

HILLTOP HOUSE
Box 806
Harpers Ferry, West Virginia 25425
(304) 535-6321
Innkeeper: D.D. Kilham

Hilltop House is a stone and white frame building that sits high above the town of Harpers Ferry, offering a spectacular view of three states as well as the confluence of the Potomac and Shenandoah Rivers. The inn was built in 1888 and during its heyday was a favorite summer destination of Woodrow Wilson, Alexander Graham Bell and Mark Twain.

The present owner, D.D. Kilham, formerly a Baltimore attorney, purchased the building in 1955. Kilham's ancestors were some of the earliest settlers around Harpers Ferry, and the plight of the once stately inn caught his attention while he was visiting relatives in the area.

"The building had been virtually abandoned," Kilham recalls. Rather than attempting a prohibitively expensive restoration, Kilham chose to modernize the building. Over the years he has installed private baths in all 50 rooms and built several additional dining areas as well as conference rooms. Despite the changes the big, rambling building still retains its 19th century feel.

The dining room serves a variety of family style dinners, and the specialty is fried chicken prepared in a manner Kilham himself developed. "It's a process that keeps the inside moist while giving it a crunchy exterior."

Although the old inn has undergone many changes over the years, the magnificent view has remained the same; and the town of Harpers Ferry, now a National Historic Park, is a fascinating place to spend an afternoon. A variety of audio-visual programs tell the story of John Brown's raid, and a short hike takes one to Jefferson Rock for a stunning view which Thomas Jefferson described as "worth a voyage across the Atlantic."

Season: Closed December 15th through January 15th.

Dining: Dining room serves three meals daily to public.

Children: Welcome.

Pets: Not permitted.

Payment: Visa & personal check.

Directions: Off Rt. 340 on Ridge Street in Harpers Ferry.

Rates: $36, double occupancy.

Lewisburg

THE GENERAL LEWIS INN
301 E. Washington Street
Lewisburg, West Virginia 24901
(304) 645-2600
Innkeeper: John McIlhenny

The oldest portion of the General Lewis Inn was built in 1834 as a private residence. Randolph Hock purchased the house in 1928, added a wing of guest rooms and opened the inn, which is still operated by the Hock family.

Located on a tree-lined street in the heart of Lewisburg, the grounds have witnessed a great deal of history, including a Civil War battle, as well as an unsuccessful slave revolt led by a slave named Reuben. Reuben was tried and hanged in 1861, but his tiny log cabin still stands at the rear of the inn.

Lewisburg boasts an unusually large number of antebellum buildings, and a self-guided tour of the historic district is available. "Lewisburg is a charming town that has remained remarkably unchanged," says innkeeper John McIlhenny. "We are surrounded by beautiful mountain scenery and under-utilized state parks. We encourage our guests to explore the area. We'll even pack picnic lunches on request."

Antique lovers will delight in the inn's furnishings, including a nickelodeon that still serenades guests. The front desk, hand built of walnut and pine, dates from 1760. Thomas Jefferson and Patrick Henry both registered at the desk when it was in the Sweet Chalybeate Springs Hotel, which is no longer standing. Most of the antiques are not simply for show. Says McIlhenny, "There isn't a bed in the inn that isn't over 100 years old."

Season: Open year round.
Dining: Dining room serves three meals daily to public.
Children: Welcome.
Pets: Permitted.
Payment: American Express, Visa, MasterCard & personal check.
Directions: Just off I-64 in downtown Lewisburg.
Rates: Range from $35 to $50, double occupancy.

White Sulphur Springs

THE GREENBRIER
White Sulphur Springs, West Virginia 24986
(304) 536-1110

The Greenbrier, one of the east's most exclusive resorts, traces its history back to the early 1800s. The sulphur springs located on the grounds have long drawn invalids, sightseers and vacationers. The Greenbriers' immediate forerunner was "The Old White," one of the social centers of the south before the Civil War. After the war "The Old White" became the summer home of Robert E. Lee.

The central portion of the present hotel was erected in 1910, and many additions have been made since then. "The Old White" was demolished in 1922 because it did not meet modern fire codes, but the tradition of gracious southern hospitality lives on.

The resort offers every sort of recreation imaginable on its 6,500-acre holdings. Guest houses, distinct from the hotel itself, are available and most of them date back to the 19th century. One of the cottages on Baltimore Row accommodated Robert E. Lee during his visits.

Season: Open year round.

Dining: Wide variety of facilities available and open to public. Reservations required for dinner.

Children: Welcome.

Pets: Permitted only in certain cottages.

Payment: American Express, Visa, MasterCard & personal check.

Directions: Take White Sulphur Springs exit off I-64. Follow Rt. 60 for two miles.

Rates: Range from $202 to $264, double occupancy. Breakfast and dinner included in room rate. (Modified American Plan)

SKYLINE DRIVE AND THE BLUE RIDGE PARKWAY

Skyline Drive and the Blue Ridge Parkway run through the southern mountains for nearly 600 miles, giving travelers a chance to enjoy some of the most spectacular scenery in the eastern United States. Skyline Drive begins at the northern edge of the Shenandoah National Park and runs southward for a 105 miles. As the road passes out of the National Park, it becomes the Blue Ridge Parkway.

Mileposts along the Parkway are the key to knowing one's location. Milepost number one is on the Parkway's northern end at Rockfish Gap just outside of Waynesboro, Virginia, while the final milepost is near the Oconaluftee Visitor Center in the Great Smoky Mountains National Park, 469 miles to the south.

There are six inns along these scenic routes, each authorized by the National Park Service to serve those traveling along these "wilderness roads."

Dark Hollow Falls. *Shenandoah National Park, Virginia.*

THE SOUTHERN MOUNTAIN STATES
(Area of map shown below)

SKYLINE DRIVE AND THE BLUE RIDGE PARKWAY

SD—Milepost 41.7

SD—Milepost 51.3

BRP—Milepost 86

BRP—Milepost 174

BRP—Milepost 241

BRP—Milepost 408.6

Skyline Drive—Milepost 41.7

SKYLAND LODGE
P.O. Box 727
Luray, Virginia 22835
(703) 999-2211

The Skyland Lodge stands on Skyline Drive's highest point. Built in the early 1950s, the lodge complex includes motel-style units and cabins, offering a total of 158 rooms. A glass-walled dining room provides a view of the valley.
Season: Open April through late November.
Dining: All three meals served daily to public.
Children: Welcome.
Pets: Permitted.
Payment: American Express, Visa, MasterCard & personal check.
Directions: On Skyline Drive at Milepost 41.7, ten miles south of junction U.S. 211.
Rates: Range from $23.50 to $45.50, double occupancy.

Skyline Drive—Milepost 51.3

BIG MEADOW LODGE
P.O. Box 727
Luray, Virginia 22835
(703) 999-2221

The lodge sits on a high plateau overlooking the Shenandoah Valley. There are 93 guest rooms divided between the main lodge building, motel-style units, and cabins. Constructed in 1939 from stone and native chestnut, the lodge floors are of flagstone and random-width oak. On a clear day the dining room offers a 40-mile, panoramic view of the mountains reaching all the way to West Virginia.
Season: Open mid-May through October.
Dining: Three meals served daily to public.
Children: Welcome.
Pets: Permitted.
Payment: American Express, Visa, MasterCard & personal check.

Sugar Tree Lodge. *Vesuvius, Virginia.*

Directions: On Skyline Drive at Milepost 51.3, twenty miles south of junction U.S. 211.

Rates: Range from $27 to $45.50, double occupancy.

Blue Ridge Parkway—Milepost 86

PEAKS OF OTTER LODGE
P.O. Box 489
Bedford, Virginia 24523
(703) 586-1081 or (800) 542-5927

Situated in a mountain valley with tall peaks surrounding it, the lodge buildings stand alongside a large lake, a spectacular meeting of woodland and water. There are 59 guest rooms, all with private baths, and each with its own balcony or terrace. Furnishings are contemporary, and the decor throughout emphasizes natural earth tones.

The lodge restaurant's specialties include mountain trout and prime rib, and diners have a fine view of the lake while enjoying their meals.

The lodge's unusal name comes from the mountain of the same name which has long been a tourist attraction. After the Civil War, General Robert E. Lee settled in Lexington, Virginia, and occasionally visited the peaks, enjoying the grand views they provided of his beloved Virginia.

Season: Open year round.

Dining: All three meals served daily to public.

Children: Welcome.

Pets: Not permitted.

Payment: Visa, MasterCard & personal check.

Directions: On the Blue Ridge Parkway at Milepost 86 where Parkway and Rt. 43 intersect, ten miles north of Bedford.

Rates: $48, double occupancy.

Blue Ridge Parkway—Milepost 174

ROCKY KNOB CABINS
Meadows of Dan, Virginia 24120
(703) 593-3503

The cabins are furnished with two double beds, electric kitchens, running water, linens, dishes and cooking utensils. A bath house and comfort station are centrally located on the wooded grounds.
Season: Open May 30 through Labor Day.
Dining: No meals served.
Children: Welcome.
Pets: Permitted.
Payment: Visa, MasterCard & personal check.
Directions: Located on the Blue Ridge Parkway at Milepost 174.
Rates: $26, double occupancy.

Blue Ridge Parkway—Milepost 241

BLUFFS LODGE
National Park Concessions, Inc.
Laurel Springs, North Carolina 28644
(919) 372-4499

Located at a point on the Parkway known as Doughton Park, the lodge, built in 1949, stands in a highland meadow at an elevation of 3,750 feet. There are 24 guest rooms, all with private baths. Nearby is the Bluffs Coffee Shop for southern style meals including country ham and fried chicken. The Doughton Park complex also contains a photo and craft shop, as well as a service station.
Season: Open May 1 through October.
Dining: Three meals served daily to public.
Children: Welcome.
Pets: Not permitted.
Payment: Visa, MasterCard & personal check.
Directions: On the Blue Ridge Parkway at Milepost 241.
Rates: $42, double occupancy.

Trillium House. *Wintergreen, Virginia.*

Blue Ridge Parkway—Milepost 408.6

PISGAH INN
P.O. Box 749
Waynesville, North Carolina 28786
(704) 235-8228

The Pisgah Inn sits alongside the Parkway providing easy access to numerous hiking trails. A modern facility, the inn's rooms are furnished in contemporary style, all with private baths. Each room also has its own porch or balcony so that guests may enjoy spectacular views of the surrounding mountains. A gift shop and filling station complete the complex.

Season: Open May through October.
Dining: Serves three meals daily to public.
Children: Welcome.
Pets: Permitted.
Payment: Visa, MasterCard & personal check.
Directions: On Blue Ridge Parkway at Milepost 408.6.
Rates: $47, double occupancy.

For additional inns located within ten miles of the Parkway see the following entries:
Vesuvius, Virginia
Wintergreen, Virginia
Asheville, North Carolina
Balsam, North Carolina
Blowing Rock, North Carolina
Linville, North Carolina
Maggie Valley, North Carolina

Boone Tavern. *Berea, Kentucky.*

KENTUCKY

Although there are many inns located in the middle and western portions of Kentucky, Boone Tavern is the only such establishment in eastern Kentucky. (Interstate 75 which runs north-south through the state provides a convenient boundary line between the mountainous east and the bluegrass country to the west.)

While searching for Kentucky inns I queried a number of Kentuckians who mentioned several reasons for the absence of inns in the area. First, eastern Kentucky contains no cities of any size. Middlesboro, with a population of only 12,000, is by far the largest city, and towns like Harlan (pop. 3,000) are more typical.

A second factor is the absence of an interstate through the region. The Daniel Boone Parkway, a modern, divided highway runs into the heart of the mountains, but terminates at the small coal town of Hazard.

For the present, small mom and pop motels (varying widely in quality) reign supreme. Sniffed one eastern Kentuckian when I inquired about inns, "We don't have inns up here." Adding with a friendly wink, "If I was you, I'd go check with them poshy bluegrass folks."

THE SOUTHERN MOUNTAIN STATES
(Area of map shown below)

KENTUCKY

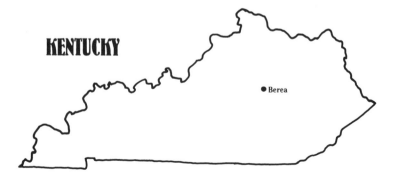

• Berea

Berea

BOONE TAVERN
CPO 2345
Berea, Kentucky 40404
(606) 986-9358
Innkeeper: Miriam R. Pride

Boone Tavern is owned and operated by Berea College, a four-year
liberal arts college dedicated to serving the residents of Appalachia.
Founded by abolitionists in the mid 1850s, the college has a long
history of social action which has led to some unique policies. To
gain admission, a student must be a resident of Appalachia from a
low-income family, making Berea the only college in America where
students are turned away because they have too *much* money.

Another Berea trademark is its mandatory work program, designed
to help students meet expenses. Boone Tavern's staff is composed
primarily of Berea students, many of whom are majoring in hotel/
restaurant management.

"Boone Tavern was founded in 1909 as a guest house for the
college," explains Miriam Pride, the general manager. "After the
President's wife hosted 1500 guests in her home during one year, she
decided a guest house was a necessity."

The Tavern is known for its fine regional cooking, offering dishes
such as plantation ham with raisin sauce and fresh rhubarb pie.
Meals are served in several sittings, and reservations are
recommended. The dining room observes a dress code that requires
coats for men, and a dress (or dress slacks) for women during dinner
and Sunday lunch.

The 57 guest rooms (all with private baths) feature furniture built
by Berea College Woodcraft, one of the many student industries that
teach students practical skills while helping them earn as they learn.
The majority of the furniture is colonial in style and the rooms are
furnished simply but tastefully.

The hotel sits at the edge of the campus, and craft enthusiasts will
find numerous galleries featuring Appalachian crafts within walking
distance. The Tavern itself has a shop in the lobby featuring student
handicrafts. Nearby is the Berea College Appalachian Museum, a

collection of photos and artifacts depicting mountain culture. Guided tours of the campus and student industries are available.

Season: Open year round.

Dining: All three meals served to public daily.

Children: Welcome.

Pets: Permitted.

Payment: American Express, Visa, MasterCard, Diner's Club, & personal check.

Directions: Take exit 76 off I-75. Go east into Berea to third traffic light. Turn right.

Rates: Range from $28 to $45, double occupancy.

Hale Springs Inn. *Rogersville, Tennessee.*

TENNESSEE

Gatlinburg

BUCKHORN INN
Rt. 3
Gatlinburg, Tennessee 37738
(615) 436-4668
Innkeepers: Robert and Rachel Young and Kathy Welch

The Buckhorn Inn sits on a quiet hilltop six miles from the hustle and bustle of Gatlinburg. From the inn's front porch one has a spectacular view of Mount LeConte, one of the highest peaks in the Smokies.

Built in 1938, the inn was one of the first guest facilities to appear after the creation of the Great Smoky Mountains National Park. The present owners, Robert and Rachel Young, purchased the inn and the surrounding wooded acres from its original owner, and they have maintained the Buckhorn's tradition of quiet hospitality.

Stepping into the Buckhorn's large front parlor is like entering a private home. A grand piano stands in one corner, bookcases line one wall, and original artwork hangs throughout the building—a reflection of Rachel's career as an artist and art historian.

There are seven guest rooms in the main building (all with private

THE SOUTHERN MOUNTAIN STATES
(Area of map shown below)

baths) as well as four cottages on the grounds. The inn is furnished with a mixture of antiques and contemporary pieces, creating a homey, lived-in atmosphere.

Breakfast and dinner are served at one end of the large parlor. Its doors open onto the long front porch. A small man-made pond, stocked with brim and bass is just a short walk down the wooded slope. Guests are welcome to try their luck at fishing (no license needed) or simply to snooze in the hammock strung under the trees.

Season: Open April through November.

Dining: Breakfast and dinner served to public, by reservation only.

Children: No children under six, please.

Pets: Not permitted.

Payment: No credit cards. Personal checks accepted.

Directions: Follow U.S. 441 into Gatlinburg and turn onto Highway 73/321 east. Follow 73/321 for approximately five miles and turn left onto Buckhorn Road. Proceed one mile to Tudor Mountain Road and take a right. Inn is short distance up the hill.

Rates: Range from $74 to $90, double occupancy. Breakfast and dinner included in room rate.

LECONTE LODGE
P.O. Box 350
Gatlinburg, Tennessee 37738
(615) 436-4473
Innkeepers: Jim Huff and Tim Line

A stay at LeConte Lodge is a truly unique experience. Situated on Mt. LeConte (elevation 6,593 ft.) in the Great Smoky Mountains National Park, the lodge is the highest guest facility in the eastern United States, offering breathtaking views of the surrounding wilderness. There are *no* roads up the mountain. Guests reach the lodge by hiking one of five trails, ranging from five and a half to eight miles in length.

After spending four to five hours climbing the mountain, the rustic lodge buildings are a welcome slice of civilization. Eight cabins and two larger lodge structures provide accommodations (primarily double bunk beds) for 40 people, a limit imposed by the National Park Service.

The lodge was built before the creation of the National Park, and the Park Service has allowed it to remain in operation because the owner, Jim Huff, takes extraordinary measures not to disturb the mountain's delicate ecological balance.

For years, supplies were packed up the mountain on horseback; but when it became evident that the horse's hooves were eroding the trails, Huff solved the problem by purchasing three llamas. The light footed animals make three trips each week, carrying perishables up the mountain, and packing all non-burnable garbage back down. Each spring, the bulk of the supplies (over 50 tons) are delivered by helicopter.

There is no electricity and fires are not allowed, so cabins are heated by kerosene stoves, and propane is used for cooking. Meals are served family style in a separate dining hall and the dinner menu hasn't changed in 20 years: minestrone soup, Argentine beef and gravy, green beans, baked apples, mashed potatoes, and for dessert, half a canned peach.

"It's a good hearty meal that satisfies hikers' appetites," says Huff. "When you sit down to dinner, after hiking up the mountain, I guarantee you'll remember this meal as one of the best you've ever eaten."

Season: Open April through October. Reservations are mandatory.
Dining: Meals served to overnight guests only.
Children: Welcome.
Pets: Not permitted.
Payment: Prepayment required to confirm reservation. No credit cards. Personal checks accepted.
Directions: Parking available at each trailhead. Stop at Park Visitor Center for directions.
Rates: $33 *per person*, $22 for children under ten. Breakfast and dinner included in room rate. Lunch is available only for those staying more than one night.

MOUNTAIN VIEW HOTEL
P.O. Box 727
Gatlinburg, Tennessee 37738
(615) 436-4132
Innkeepers: Jack Huff, Tom and Jane Woods

It's hard to imagine the town of Gatlinburg as a sleepy mountain village with cornfields, frame farm houses, and pastures stretching alongside the Little Pigeon River; but that was the scene in 1916 when Andrew Jackson Huff built the original Mountain View Hotel on what is now Gatlinburg's main street.

Huff was a lumberman who began boarding the salesmen traveling into the remote lumber camps, and then decided the town needed a guest house. The original Mountain View was the first hotel in Gatlinburg and had only ten rooms. By 1926 it had grown to 50 rooms which were rented for the sum of $3 a night.

Tom Woods has managed the Mountain View for 35 years and has witnessed the dramatic changes Gatlinburg has undergone. "Thirty-five years ago there were only four hotels in the entire town," says Tom. "I used to practice my golf shots on the hotel's front lawn, and if I was driving well I'd hit the balls into a corn field."

The lawn is now a municipal parking lot, and restaurants and shops surround the Mountain View, but much of the old flavor remains. Numerous additions over the years, including a clock tower which houses an elevator, have given the exterior a deceptively modern look, but once one steps through the broad front doors into the lobby, it's easy to forget the hustle and bustle outside.

The inn still owns 30 acres, and there are two swimming pools on the property. The 75 guest rooms, all with private baths, contain furniture handmade by local craftsmen, while a few of the original furnishings (now antiques) are scattered throughout the building. Some of the rooms still have cherry corner cupboards, once the only "closets" available.

In the 1960s a motor lodge was built on the slopes behind the hotel, providing 40 additional rooms, all with private baths and decorated in contemporary style.

Season: Open year round.
Dining: Dining room will be closed during early part of 1985 for extensive renovations. Service will resume at undetermined date.
Children: Welcome.

Pets: Permitted.
Payment: American Express, Visa, MasterCard, Diner's Club, Carte Blanche & personal check.
Directions: Follow Route 441 into Gatlinburg. Hotel is on 441 next to the Chamber of Commerce building.
Rates: Range from $25 to $45, double occupancy.

THE WONDERLAND HOTEL
Gatlinburg, Tennessee 37738
(615) 436-5490
Innkeeper: Darrell Huskey

maybe

The main reason for a stay at The Wonderland is its location: seven miles from Gatlinburg within the boundaries of the Great Smoky Mountains National Park.

Built in 1912, the rambling white frame structure was originally the property of a private club where members and their guests could enjoy a mountain vacation. When the National Park came into being, club members were paid 50¢ on every dollar appraised, and were given a lifetime lease.

In 1972, the remaining club members arranged a new 20- year lease with the Park Service, so the Wonderland's survival is assured until 1992.

The two-story hotel has wide verandas well supplied with rockers. The swift, rockfilled Little River flows in front of the building, and Elkmont Campground, one of the Park's most popular facilities, is just up the road.

Despite its prime location, the Wonderland is not for those accustomed to posh accommodations. The exterior is badly in need of a coat of paint, and the hotel's 27 guest rooms are filled with a hodge podge of furniture, everything from antiques to contemporary pieces. The majority have private baths but there are no phones, TVs or radios—facts which will please some guests and dismay others.

The Wonderland serves three meals daily to the public, and the menu includes southern fried fish and chicken as well as sandwiches, at inexpensive prices.
Season: Open Memorial Day weekend through October.
Dining: Three meals served daily to public.
Children: Welcome.
Pets: Not permitted.

Payment: Visa, MasterCard & personal check.
Directions: Once inside National Park, follow signs to Elkmont Camp-
ground. Inn will be on left just before campground.
Rates: Range from $32 to $60, double occupancy.

Kingsport

SHALLOWFORD FARM, B. & B.
Rt. 6, Box 142
Kingsport, Tennessee 37660
(615) 245-0798
Innkeeper: Jane Walley

To reach Shallowford Farm one drives along a narrow country road
winding across the bluffs that overlook the Ho' on River just outside
the city of Kingsport. The farm's tree-sh~ way passes
through pastures dotted with cattle mile before reaching
the Walley family's secluded ho~
   "We gave up searching home to restore and built this
house in 1979," expl~ Walley. "The house has an 'old' feel
because we used based on a home from the colonial period."
   The house is furnished with antiques ranging from primitive to
Victorian. Old trunks, brass beds, marble top dressers, and wooden
shutters all add to the home's relaxed country style. The two guest
rooms are upstairs and share a bath just down the hall.
   Guests are welcome to enjoy the farm's well-kept grounds, taking a
dip in the swimming pool or a stroll through Jane's expanding herb
garden. The farm's 47 acres are home to a herd of beef cattle,
poultry, dogs, cats, several horses and a peacock.
   The Walleys began offering B. & B. accommodations in 1982.
"We're very low key," Jane says. "On the occasions when all the
children are home from college we don't have room for guests, and I
just have to say so." For those fortunate enough to find a room
available, the Walleys offer a full breakfast featuring farm-fresh eggs.
Season: Open year round.
Dining: No meals served to public.
Children: Welcome.
Pets: Permitted by special arrangement only.
Payment: No credit cards. Personal checks accepted.

Shallowford Farm, B.&B. *Kingsport, Tennessee.*

Directions: Please phone for directions. Map mailed to guests on re-
ceipt of one night's deposit.
Rates: $30, double occupancy. Full breakfast included in room rate.

Knoxville

THREE CHIMNEYS
1302 White Avenue
Knoxville, Tennessee 37916
(615) 521-4970
Innkeepers: Margo and Alfred Akerman, Marion and
Beau Hannifin

Three Chimneys is located in a section of Knoxville known as Fort
Sanders, so-called because of an earth-work fort constructed on its
heights during the Civil War. Pulitzer prize-winning author James
Agee grew up several blocks away. His poignant novel, *A Death in the
Family,* describes life in the neighborhood at the turn of the century.
Three Chimneys, a Queen Anne mansion built in 1896, would have
been familiar to the young Agee.

The main campus of the University of Tennessee wraps around the
home. Any on-campus events are within walking distance, and one
block east is the site of the 1982 World's Fair. Although the fair is long
since over, several fine restaurants operate on the site and the Fair
grounds, complete with a man-made lake, are a pleasant place for an
evening stroll.

The inn has four guest rooms, each named for mountain
wildflowers or plants. Furnished with antiques, the rooms also have
fresh flowers, a fruit basket and imported English toffee awaiting
guests upon their arrival. Two of the rooms have private baths; the
other two share a water closet and separate bath just a few steps
down the hall. Guests have access to the home through a private side
entrance so they may come and go as they please.

A full country breakfast (including homemade buttermilk biscuits
and grits) is served in a glassed-in side porch, and a morning paper
is provided so guests may keep up with the news over a leisurely cup
of coffee.
Season: Open year round.
Dining: No meals served to the public.

Children: Welcome.
Pets: Not permitted.
Payment: No credit cards. Personal checks accepted.
Directions: In Knoxville, take 17th Street exit (number 387) off I-40.
Go south on 17th toward the University of Tennessee. After three-
way stop at top of hill, proceed one block and turn left onto White
Avenue. Inn is three blocks down, on the right.
Rates: Range from $40 to $50. Full breakfast included in room rate.

Rogersville

THE HALE SPRINGS INN
110 West Main Street
Rogersville, Tennessee 37857
(615) 272-5171
Innkeepers: Carl Netherland-Brown and Lola Moore

Built in 1824, the Hale Springs Inn is Tennessee's oldest continuously
operated inn and was an important stop on the stagecoach road that
ran from Nashville to Washington, D.C. Andrew Jackson lived at the
inn as a young lawyer, and two other Presidents, Andrew Johnson
and James K. Polk, were guests.

A massive restoration, begun in 1982, has returned the inn to its
19th century elegance. The original heart-pine floors and handmade
nails have been exposed, and the guest rooms furnished with
antiques. Six of the seven guest rooms have working fireplaces, and
generous amounts of wood are supplied so guests can enjoy a cozy
fire.

Private baths have replaced the row of six privies that originally
stood in the courtyard behind the building. "We're an interpretive
restoration," one employee explained. "If we'd done an *exact*
restoration visitors would say, 'Gee, I'd love to take a tour—but I
think I'll stay at the Ramada!'"

Rogersville has the slow paced feel of many small southern towns,
and the area is steeped in history. Not far from the inn, Crockett's
Creek meanders past a tiny cemetery where Davy Crockett's
grandparents lie buried, the victims of a 1777 Indian massacre.
Season: Open year round.
Dining: Three meals served daily to public.

Children: Welcome.
Pets: Permitted.
Payment: American Express, Visa, MasterCard & personal check.
Directions: Located on 11W in downtown Rogersville.
Rates: Range from $35 to $55, double occupancy.

Rugby

PIONEER COTTAGE & NEWBURY HOUSE OF HISTORIC RUGBY
P.O. Box 8
Rugby, Tennessee 37733
(615) 628-2441

The community of Rugby was founded in 1880 by Englishman
Thomas Hughes, the author of *Tom Brown's Schooldays*, as a
cooperative venture for the younger sons of the English gentry.
Excluded from inheriting the family fortune because of the custom of
primogeniture, these young men were kept from pursuing many
careers because of social pressure. Hughes set out to provide a
supportive environment for these well-educated, but penniless,
gentlemen.

Rugby flourished as a resort community during the 1880s, but a
series of disasters, including a typhoid epidemic and confusion with
land titles, sent many of the British colonists packing.

Today, 17 of the original Victorian structures remain, and several
are open to the public: Christ Church; Hughes' home, Kingstone
Lisle; and the Hughes Public Library with its original collection of
Victorian literature.

Pioneer Cottage, the first frame structure in town, is available for
overnight guests. The period furnishings include several pieces that
belonged to the British colonists, and the cottage offers a fully
equipped kitchen and three double bedrooms. For those not inclined
to cook, the Harrow Road Cafe, operated by Historic Rugby, is just
down the road.

Newbury House, the colony's first boarding house, is currently
undergoing restoration and will once again be welcoming guests after
its grand opening in May, 1985. Furnishings will be Victorian, with
five guest rooms available, three with private baths. The downstairs

parlor will serve as a tea room, and a small library, featuring publications of the period, will be accessible to guests.

Newbury House is just a short walk from the Rugby public buildings which are open from 9 a.m. to 5 p.m., Monday through Saturday, and 12 p.m. to 5 p.m. on Sunday. The Hughes library is particularly fascinating and remains virtually unchanged since it opened its doors in 1882. Its 7,000 volumes were donated to the community by 38 British and American publishers as a tribute to Thomas Hughes.

Season: Open year round.

Dining: Breakfast and lunch served to public year round. Dinner served April through October, with limited dinner service during off-season.

Children: Welcome at Pioneer Cottage. No children under six at Newbury House, please.

Pets: Not permitted.

Directions: On Highway 52, 17 miles southeast of Jamestown.

Rates: Range from $36 to $48, double occupancy. Pioneer Cottage available for $68.50 per night.

Sevierville

COVE MOUNTAIN LODGE
Route 7, Wears Valley Road
Sevierville, Tennessee 37862
In Tennessee (615) 453-6533, out of state (800)
222-1458
Innkeeper: Ellis Adams

Set on 12 acres in the shadow of Cove Mountain, the lodge is surrounded on three sides by the Great Smoky Mountains National Park. Just ten minutes from Pigeon Forge and 15 from Gatlinburg, Cove Mountain offers guests a secluded retreat with convenient access to area tourist attractions.

Built of logs taken from several East Tennessee cabins dating back to the Civil War, the lodge was constructed 25 years ago as a private residence, and since 1982 it has been the combination home/ business of Ellis Adams.

There are six guestrooms in the Adams' home; several with private entrances and private baths, as well as three efficiencies in a nearby

Blackberry Farm. *Walland, Tennessee.*

outbuilding. Most of the guest rooms have contemporary furnishings, and many of them offer stunning views of the surrounding mountains.

Adams, a native of Wears Valley, knows the ridges and hollows of the Smokies, "like the back of my hand." He is eager to share his knowledge with interested hikers, and trails on the lodge property connect with trails leading into the National Park. Adams also has ten horses which guests may rent, and guided trail rides can be arranged for the inexperienced.

For those interested in more sedentary pursuits, there is porch sitting, or strolling by the stream that runs through the property. "The major thing we offer, besides the hiking trails, is lots of privacy," says Adams. "Out here you don't hear cars, or freight trains—there's nothing but katydids."

Season: Open year round.
Dining: Full breakfast and dinner served to public by reservation only.
Children: Welcome, with prior approval.
Pets: Not permitted.
Payment: American Express, Visa, MasterCard, & personal check.
Directions: Heading south on 441 into Pigeon Forge, take a right at the first stop light onto Wears Valley Road. Drive 7½ miles to lodge sign on left. Follow gravel road 1½ miles to lodge.
Rates: Range from $25 to $50, double occupancy. Breakfast and dinner available for guests, with advance notice.

Walland

BLACKBERRY FARM
Miller's Cove Road, Rt. 1
Walland, Tennessee 37886
(615) 984-8166
Innkeepers: Gary and Bernadette Doyle

Located on 35 acres just outside the Great Smoky Mountains National Park, Blackberry Farm has been in operation since 1952, but has just recently been opened to the public. "Previously we accepted only groups," explains Bernadette Doyle, "but we are now open to the public, by reservation, from Memorial Day through Labor Day."

The inn is surrounded by the Chilhowee mountains and guests can sit on the front porch and see nothing but unspoiled countryside. Bernadette, a native New Yorker who "married into the business," admits that she had some trouble adjusting to country living. "The very first week my son was bitten by a snake when, believe it or not, he fell off his bike and landed on it." But despite some initial adjustments, Bernadette says Blackberry Farm now feels like home.

The inn's eight guestrooms, all with private baths, are decorated with antiques and each has its own style. Several of the rooms offer stunning views of the Smoky Mountains. Swimming, tennis, and a stream for fishing are available on the grounds; golf, horseback riding and the National Park, are only minutes away.

Meals at the inn are an elegant affair, with dinner served by candlelight and the table set with silver and Waterford crystal. Gary, who was trained at the Culinary Institute in New York, supervises the kitchen and serves such dishes as Roquefort stuffed sole and pork tenderloin with fruit stuffing.

Season: Memorial Day through Labor Day. (Groups accepted year round).

Dining: Dinner served to public by reservation only.

Children: Permitted by prior arrangement only.

Pets: Not permitted.

Payment: No credit cards. Personal checks accepted.

Directions: Inn is 11 miles from Jct. of 411/321 in Maryville. Follow 321 south past Walland to West Miller Cove Road. Turn right and go 3½ miles. Inn is on left.

Rates: Range from $148 to $178, double occupancy. Three meals included in room rate.

Cedar Crest: A Victorian Inn. *Asheville, North Carolina.*

NORTH CAROLINA

Asheville

CEDAR CREST: A VICTORIAN INN
674 Biltmore Avenue
Asheville, North Carolina 28803
(704) 252-1389
Innkeepers: Jack and Barbara McEwan

Cedar Crest was built in the 1890s by William E. Breese, a Confederate veteran turned banker who moved to Asheville when the small mountain town was becoming one of the county's leading summer resorts. Folks "of the better sort" were flocking to the city, and George Vanderbilt built his palatial home, Biltmore House, on an enormous estate just down the road from the Breese home.

Cedar Crest played a central role in Asheville society during the early part of the 20th century, but by the twenties the boom was over, and the stately home was turned into a sanatorium, and later a boarding house.

In 1983 Barbara McEwan was searching for a house to convert into a B. & B. inn, and happened to see Cedar Crest listed in *Preservation News*. "When we walked in the front door and saw the woodwork we knew this was it," she says.

Exquisitely carved oak woodwork greets one in the entry way, and

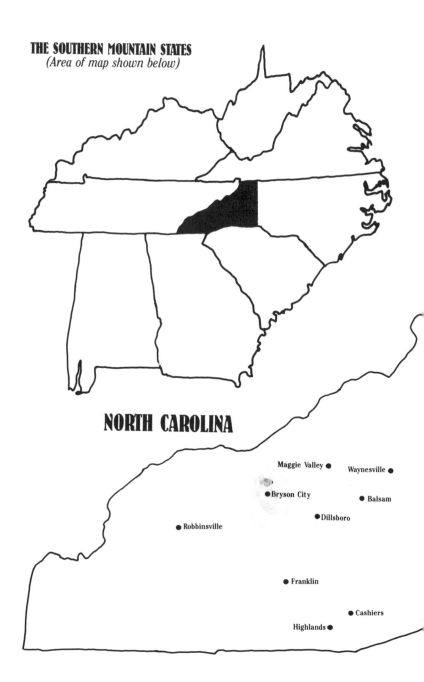

THE SOUTHERN MOUNTAIN STATES
(Area of map shown below)

NORTH CAROLINA

Maggie Valley ●   Waynesville ●

●Bryson City   ● Balsam

●Dillsboro

● Robbinsville

● Franklin

● Cashiers

Highlands ●

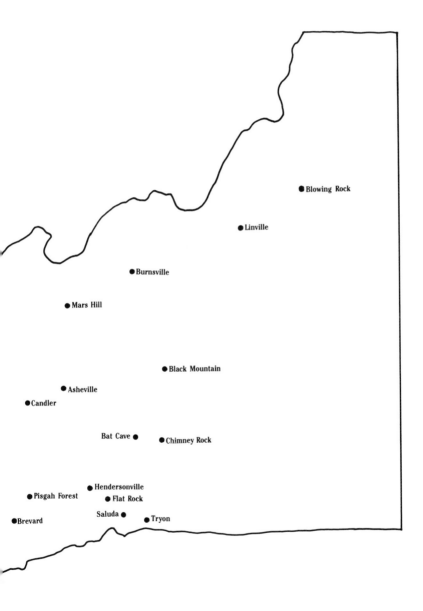

Blowing Rock

Linville

Burnsville

Mars Hill

Black Mountain

Asheville

Candler

Bat Cave

Chimney Rock

Hendersonville

Pisgah Forest

Flat Rock

Brevard

Saluda

Tryon

the entire first floor is filled with fabulous mantels and wall panels of wood, as well as a massive carved staircase leading to the upper floors. Years of dust and grime were laboriously cleaned from the wood, and visitors marvel at the delicate carving that has reappeared.

The McEwans rewired the house, put in all new plumbing, and stripped as many as 13 layers of wallpaper from the walls. Draperies and wallpapers are Victorian reproductions, and the furniture is of the period. "We've done everything as authentically as possible," says Barbara, "but we're not *high* Victorian with all the clutter. I have to live here and that would be just *too* much."

The three-story inn has 11 guest rooms, four with private baths and two with semi-private facilities. The remaining five rooms share two baths. There is a sitting area on each of the two upper floors, and the ground floor is totally open to guests, with the exception of the kitchen. (The McEwans and their three children live in the carriage house at the rear of the property.)

Guests will discover a variety of interesting details, from the third floor skylight and the guest room with a REAL featherbed, to a six-foot-long claw-footed tub. "That tub's a real treat," says Barbara. "You can stretch out and just bury yourself in bubbles."

Season: Open year round.
Dining: No meals served to the public.
Children: No small children, please.
Pets: Not permitted.
Payment: Visa, MasterCard & personal check.
Directions: Off I-40, follow signs to Biltmore House. Proceed straight ahead on Hendersonville Road/Biltmore Avenue toward town. Inn is ¼ of a mile, on the right.
Rates: Range from $45 to $60, double occupancy.

FLINT STREET INN
116 Flint Street
Asheville, North Carolina 28801
(704) 253-6723
Innkeepers: Rick and Lynne Vogel

Flint Street Inn sits on a quiet, residential street at the edge of downtown Asheville in an area known as the Montford historic district. Tall trees, a flower garden and lots of mountain laurel create the sensation of a country setting.

The Vogels are Gulf coast natives who grew tired of New Orleans' big city pace and moved to the mountains "to simplify our lifestyle." Lynn laughs at their naiveté. "With the inn, our lives are just as hectic, but in a much nicer way."

The Vogels purchased their home (built in 1915) from the family who had owned it since its construction. Some of the antiques scattered throughout the house were left by the original owners.

The inn's homey atmosphere is the product of tasteful decorating, and the fact that the Vogels are indeed welcoming you into their home. "We offer bed and breakfast accommodations, but we're different from some B. & B.s; this is my full-time job, so we're able to cater to our guests to a greater degree than many," Lynne explains.

The four guest rooms are upstairs; two have private baths, and the other two share an adjoining bath. Filled with antiques, as well as memorabilia from the twenties and thirties, each room is delightfully different.

Many small touches add to the inn's pleasing ambience; stenciled designs appear on the stairwell walls, pieces of stained glass brighten various windows, rag rugs create splashes of color on the hardwood floors, and old packing crates, rescued from the basement with labels intact, serve as end tables.

Season: Open year round.

Dining: No meals served to public.

Children: No children under 12, please.

Pets: Not permitted.

Payment: American Express & personal check.

Directions: On Flint Street, three blocks north of Asheville Civic Center.

Rates: $50, double occupancy. Full breakfast included in room rate.

GROVE PARK INN
290 Macon Avenue
Asheville, North Carolina 28804
(704) 252-2711

Amazement is the usual reaction to one's first glimpse of the Grove Park. The brainchild of Edwin Grove, a turn of the century businessman who made a fortune marketing "Bromo Quinine," the inn was built in 1912-13 of boulders hauled to the site by wagon train and laid in place by Italian stonemasons. Known for its elegance, the inn has hosted such notables as Thomas Edison, Henry Ford, the Rockefellers and F. Scott Fitzgerald.

The lobby contains two enormous fireplaces capable of burning logs up to 12 feet in length—a perfect place to gather with friends on a cold winter evening.

Over the years the inn has retained much of its original flavor while adding modern amenities. A new wing, completed in 1984, contains an indoor pool, complete health club and full conference facilities. Inn guests also have full access to the adjacent country club, including the tennis courts, pool, and 18-hole golf course.

The oldest portion of the inn has over 140 guest rooms which feature the building's original oak furniture: the new wings, with more than 200 rooms, have contemporary furnishings.

There are a variety of dining facilities, but the most memorable is the Sunset Terrace, an informal dining area with wonderful views of Asheville and the mountains that ring the city.

Season: Open year round.

Dining: A variety of dining facilities serve three meals daily to the public.

Children: Welcome.

Pets: Not permitted, but arrangements for kenneling may be made in advance.

Payment: American Express, Visa, MasterCard & personal check.

Directions: Take I-240 to Charlotte Street exit. Go north on Charlotte ½ mile. Entrance will be on left.

Rates: Range from $75 to $110, double occupancy.

THE RAY HOUSE, BED AND BREAKFAST
83 Hillside Street
Asheville, North Carolina 28801
(704) 252-0106
Innkeepers: Alice and Will Curtis

The Ray House, built around the turn of the century by one of Asheville's leading families, sits on a tree-shaded acre just minutes away from downtown Asheville. The University of North Carolina's Botanical Gardens are within easy walking distance.

The Curtises are a gregarious couple who have combined two dreams: restoring an old house and opening a guest house. When they found the Ray House, "We just jumped right in," laughs Alice. "We're learning as we go, but the house is coming along."

The three guest rooms are upstairs. One has a private bath/kitchen, and the other two rooms share a bath. The rooms are furnished with antiques the Curtises refinished themselves, and the home's many windows make the interior light and inviting.

Each room has been given a name related to Asheville's cultural history: The Thomas Wolfe room, O. Henry room and the Bartok room. The Curtises are more than happy to be your "arm-chair guides," and their enthusiasm for their town is infectious.

Season: Open year round.

Dining: No meals served to public.

Children: Welcome.

Pets: Not permitted.

Payment: No credit cards. Personal checks accepted.

Directions: From I-240 in Asheville, take Merriman Avenue exit onto Highway 25 north. Go to second traffic light. Turn left onto Hillside.

Rates: Range from $37 to $42, double occupancy. Continental breakfast included in room rate.

THE OLD REYNOLDS MANSION
100 Reynolds Heights
Asheville, North Carolina 28804
(704) 254-0496
Innkeepers: Fred and Helen Faber

This massive three-story brick mansion was built before the Civil War by Colonel Daniel Reynolds. Colonel Reynolds had ten children, five boys and five girls, but even that large family could easily be accommodated in the mansion's nearly 7,000 square feet. (The porches that wrap around the house on two levels add an additional 4,000 square feet.)

The house remained in the Reynolds family until the early 1970s, but when Fred and Helen Faber first saw it in 1977 it was in an alarming state of disrepair. "People thought it was too far gone," Fred recalls. "Everybody thought we were crazy for tackling it."

At the time of the purchase Fred's job was in Minnesota, so for several years the Fabers' work on the house was limited. "We'd come down in the summers to prop up the porches," says Fred. In 1981

Fred quit his company job, they moved into the house and the work began in earnest.

Today, the 17 room house sits on its four-acre knoll in renewed splendour. There are ten guest rooms, three with private baths, with the remaining rooms sharing three baths. There are eight working fireplaces in the house, four of them in guest rooms. Helen's masterful sense of color and design is evident throughout; wallpaper, carpets, and antiques blend beautifully. A large 1930s swimming pool at the rear of the house was reclaimed from dense underbrush. "We had to mow it before we could fix it," Fred laughs.

The Fabers are justifiably proud of their restoration. Says Fred with a twinkle, "Helen always wanted a southern mansion with white pillars. Well, now she's got 27 pillars."

Season: Open year round.

Dining: No meals served to public.

Children: Welcome.

Pets: Not permitted.

Payment: No credit cards. Personal checks accepted.

Directions: In Asheville, take the Merrimon Avenue exit off I-240. Follow Rt. 25 north past Beaver Lake. Turn right, just past stop light, on Beaver Street. Turn left up gravel lane.

Rates: Range from $25 to $47, double occupancy. Continental breakfast included in room rate.

Balsam

BALSAM LODGE
Box 279
Balsam, North Carolina 28707
(704) 456-6528
Innkeepers: Marie and Gordie Pike

This bed and breakfast lodge was opened in 1983 with accommodations available in a turn of the century farm house or Balsam's original railroad depot, relocated to a site behind the main house. The depot's four rooms have kitchens as well as private baths, and the four rooms in the upstairs of the main house share a bath at the end of the hall.

Mrs. Pike lives on the first floor and provides guests with a continental breakfast featuring homemade muffins and biscuits. When not busy greeting guests, she goes to auctions and craft fairs, searching for items to enhance the lodge's country flavor.

Season: Open May through October.

Dining: No meals served to public.

Children: Welcome.

Pets: Permitted in depot, but not in house.

Payment: No credit cards. Personal checks accepted.

Directions: Take Balsam exit off U.S. 19A/23. Follow signs to lodge.

Rates: Range from $25 to $35, double occupancy. Continental breakfast included in room rate.

THE BALSAM MOUNTAIN INN
P.O. Box 40
Balsam, North Carolina 28707
(704) 456-9498
Innkeepers: Don, Elizabeth, Bob & Sara LaBrant

This turn of the century inn rambles across a high hill overlooking the tiny hamlet of Balsam. The town has practically disappeared, but the three-story inn, built in 1906, is still very much alive.

The LaBrant family has run the inn for 16 years, and are fighting their own personal war against inflation. They pride themselves on the fact that their coffee is still only 5¢ a cup. Explains Elizabeth LaBrant, "We believe people should get their money's worth."

Breakfast and dinner, included in the room rate, are served family-style in the large, columned dining room. A massive buffet at one end of the room, part of the inn's original furnishings, is still in use. Chef Bob LaBrant provides a hearty fare sure to satisfy even the hungriest diner. For lunch, Bob keeps two types of homemade soup simmering and guests help themselves. Payment is on the honor system, with guests working the cash register.

There are no fancy recreational facilities, but there are 26 acres of woodland to roam, or games of croquet or shuffleboard to play. "The biggest thrill we have at the Balsam," teases Elizabeth, "is not turning over in our wicker rockers." The inn's loyal clientele don't appear to mind; they are too busy enjoying a taste of the past at yesterday's prices.

Season: Open mid-June through Labor Day.

Dining: Breakfast and dinner served to public by reservation.

Children: Permitted, but not encouraged.

Pets: Not permitted.

Payment: No credit cards. Personal checks accepted.

Directions: Take Balsam exit off U.S. 19A/23. Follow signs ¼ mile to inn.

Rates: $43, double occupancy. Breakfast and dinner included in room rate.

Bat Cave

STONEHEARTH INN
P.O. Box 9
Bat Cave, North Carolina 28710
(704) 625-9990
Innkeepers: Don and Ellen Staley

This tiny inn clings to the banks of rushing, rock-filled Broad River. The building has served as just about everything you can imagine: post office, antique shop, and a real rip-snorting road house. It was purchased in 1980 by Don and Ellen Staley, midwesterners who fell in love with the mountains.

The inn has three floors. The Staleys and their four children live on the top floor, the restaurant occupies the second, and the four guest rooms, each with private bath, are downstairs, overlooking the river. They are furnished in cheery American country style.

The atmosphere is very casual. Guests help themselves to a continental breakfast, and may come and go as they please through a downstairs entrance. The restaurant serves only the evening meal. Ellen does all the cooking with the children pitching in. "This business has been great for the kids," says Don. "They've come to understand that material things don't just magically appear—someone has to put in a tremendous amount of work."

Season: Open year round.

Dining: Dining room open seasonally. Dinner served to public on Friday and Saturday only. Reservations suggested.

Children: Welcome.

Pets: Not permitted.

Payment: Visa, MasterCard & personal check.

Directions: On Highway 74 in "downtown" Bat Cave.

Rates: $25, double occupancy. Continental breakfast included in room rate.

Black Mountain

THE RED ROCKER INN
136 N. Dougherty Street
Black Mountain, North Carolina 28711
(704) 669-5991
Innkeepers: Pat & Fred Eshleman

The cheerful red rockers that line the inn's front porch reflect the relaxed atmosphere innkeeper Fred Eshleman creates for his guests. He and his wife have been avid country inn goers for years, and considered 35 inns that were on the market before purchasing the Red Rocker in 1982. "We've pooled what we thought was best from the inns where we've stayed." The result is delightful.

Each of the 18 guest rooms is unique. The decor is turn of the century, with white ruffled Priscilla curtains, claw-footed tubs and ceiling fans. Nearly every room has a private bath.

The inn was built in 1894 by farmer Silas Dougherty as a wedding gift for his daughter, and was opened as an inn almost immediately, operating as the Dougherty Heights Inn until the mid-1970s. "When we bought the inn *everything* was painted red, white and blue," says Eshleman with a pained look.

The inn's no-TV, no-phone philosophy encourages guests to talk to one another, and Eshleman intentionally acquired large round tables so, in his words, "strangers could meet over a good meal." The evening meal is served family-style with two seatings, one at 5:30 and one at 7:30. The meal commences with a welcome and a blessing by the innkeeper. The menu changes daily, but always features homemade breads and mouth watering desserts.

The inn's philosophy of creating a relaxed atmosphere for guests keeps the inn's staff on the run, but the innkeeper can be located easily even at the busiest times. In the entry way sits a bell with a sign attached which reads, "If you need the innkeeper, please ring."
Season: Open April 15 through October 31.
Dining: Country breakfast, a la carte lunch, and family-style evening meal served to public. Reservations suggested. (No evening meal is

The Red Rocker Inn. *Black Mountain, North Carolina.*

served on Sunday).
Children: Welcome.
Pets: Not permitted.
Payment: No credit cards. Personal checks accepted.
Directions: In Black Mountain, turn left onto 70 West. Take right at first traffic light onto Dougherty Street.
Rates: Range from $30 to $45, double occupancy.

Blowing Rock

THE FARM HOUSE
P.O. Box 126
Blowing Rock, North Carolina 28605
(704) 295-7361
Innkeepers: E.J. and Shirley Blackwell

Built in 1893, this inn was originally known as the Skyland because of its location overlooking the magnificent scenery of the John's River Gorge. The Blackwell family purchased the inn some 40 years ago and have run it as a summer resort ever since.

The sprawling frame building is a showcase of Victorian antiques, and most of the rooms are furnished with period pieces. Three types of accommodations are available; 12 rooms in the inn itself, all with private baths, as well as cottages and several modern motel-style units.

The inn's dining room is staffed by singing waiters and waitresses (college music students) who entertain diners. "It's very popular with our guests," says Shirley Blackwell. Live entertainment has been a tradition at the inn for 29 years. "I was one of the first singing waitresses," laughs Shirley, "and I wound up marrying the innkeeper's son."
Season: Open Memorial Day through Labor Day.
Dining: Breakfast served to guests only. Lunch and dinner served to public daily.
Children: Welcome.
Pets: Permitted in cottages only.
Payment: No credit cards. Personal checks accepted.
Directions: Just off South/Business 321 in Blowing Rock.
Rates: Range from $40 to $75, double occupancy.

GREEN PARK INN
P.O. Box 7
Blowing Rock, North Carolina 28605
(704) 295-3141
Innkeepers: Pat and Allen McCain

Bright green shutters and a life-size green horse harnessed to an old surrey greet guests as they arrive at the Green Park Inn. This popular resort was built in 1882 adjacent to the famous landmark from which Blowing Rock gets its name. (The large outcropping has natural updrafts that cause light objects tossed off it to float upward.)

The 74-room inn is furnished with pieces from the Victorian period. Fine wicker furniture is a tradition at the inn, and has inspired "The Green Park Collection," a new line of wicker now being marketed nationally.

The inn sits astride the Eastern Continental Divide at an elevation of 4,300 feet, making summers delightfully cool. A variety of recreational opportunities are offered, including golf, swimming, and tennis. The inn is also a perfect base of operations for ski enthusiasts since six ski resorts are located within a few miles. From May to mid-October, additional entertainment is provided by the Green Park dinner theatre, as well as frequent dances featuring the "Big Band" sound.

Season: Open early May through January 1.
Dining: Three meals served daily to public.
Children: Welcome.
Pets: Not permitted, but arrangements for kenneling may be made in advance.
Payment: American Express, Visa, MasterCard & personal check.
Directions: On South 321 in Blowing Rock.
Rates: Rates range from $60 to $135, double occupancy.

MAPLE LODGE
P.O. Box 66
Blowing Rock, North Carolina 28605
(704) 295-3331
Innkeepers: Jack and Rheba Crane

Maple Lodge provides homey bed and breakfast accommodations in the resort town of Blowing Rock. Built in the 1940s, the white frame house is shaded by two huge maples in the front yard. Rustic willow furniture on the front porch and under the trees offer perfect places to relax after a morning of browsing through Blowing Rock's craft and specialty shops.

The comfortably furnished guest rooms are upstairs and all have private baths. Downstairs, two parlors and a TV room are also for guests' use. At the rear of the house, a stone patio has been glassed in and a wood-burning stove added for cool fall evenings. In summer, a colorful flower garden delights visitors.

Season: Open April through October.
Dining: No meals served to public.
Children: Welcome.
Pets: Not permitted.
Payment: No credit cards. Personal checks accepted.
Directions: One-half block off Main Street on Sunset Drive.
Rates: $50, double occupancy. Continental breakfast included in room rate.

THE RAGGED GARDEN
Sunset Drive, P.O. Box 1927
Blowing Rock, North Carolina 28605
(704) 295-9703
Innkeepers: Joe and Joyce Villani

Opened in April of 1983, the Ragged Garden sits just off Main Street on a quiet acre filled with huge trees, rhododendron and roses. The old house stood empty for several years before its recent renovation. The ground floor has been transformed into a restaurant serving classic cuisine with a northern Italian emphasis; a variety of veal dishes, as well as pasta, highlight the menu. Owner/chef, Joe Villani, has operated several fine restaurants in New England and Florida, and received his early training at New York's famed Sardi's.

Upstairs, five bedrooms (all with private baths) are available. The rooms are tastefully decorated with a mixture of antiques and country classics.

Season: Open during summer season with limited operation in winter. Phone for exact dates.

Dining: Dinner served to public. Reservations suggested.

Children: No children under twelve, please.

Pets: Not permitted.

Payment: American Express, Visa, MasterCard & personal check.

Directions: One block off Main Street in downtown Blowing Rock.

Rates: $60, double occupancy. Continental breakfast included in room rate.

SUNSHINE INN
P.O. Box 528, Sunset Drive
Blowing Rock, North Carolina 28605
(704) 295-3487
Innkeepers: Jim and Sue Byrne

This comfortable frame guest house has been the home/business of Jim and Sue Byrne since 1980. Jim is a former corporate executive who turned to innkeeping because he wanted to spend more time with his family. While many inns are unprepared for children, the Byrnes, with five children of their own, welcome child guests. "We're family oriented," smiles Sue.

There are seven guest rooms. Three have private baths; the other four share one bath. The rooms are decorated with quilt wall hangings, throw rugs and antiques. Sue's needlework hangs throughout the house and a doll shop fills one downstairs room.

Just down the hall is the dining room where Sue serves hearty, family-style meals. The menu changes daily and is posted on a blackboard on the front porch. The Byrnes are often up at five a.m. to begin breakfast preparations and they rarely close the kitchen before ten in the evening, but the dining room is closed on Sunday evenings and all day Mondays, providing a respite from the hectic pace. (Rooms are still available for overnight guests on those days.)

Season: Open May through October.

Dining: Breakfast and dinner served to public. Breakfast only on Sunday. Dining room is closed on Monday.

Children: Welcome.

Pets: Not permitted.
Payment: Visa, MasterCard & personal check.
Directions: Two blocks off Main Street on Sunset Drive.
Rates: Range from $29 to $40, double occupancy. Continental breakfast included in room rate every day except Sunday.

Brevard

THE INN AT BREVARD
410 E. Main Street
Brevard, North Carolina 28712
(704) 884-2105
Innkeepers: Bertrand and Eileen Bourget

The Inn at Brevard, known for many years as the Colonial Inn, was built around the turn of the century as the home of William Breese, Jr., a prominent businessman and mayor of Brevard. The Breese family had close ties to the Confederacy and in 1911 the white mansion was the site of a reunion of Stonewall Jackson's troops, with Mrs. Jackson in attendance. The residence was converted into an inn during the 1940s and had a succession of owners until purchased by the Bourgets in 1984.

The newly refurbished mansion has been furnished with antiques, and its heavy, white columns and hanging balcony make for a stunning exterior. There are two guest rooms (with a shared bath) on the second floor. The first floor has a sitting room, TV room, and dining area. Most of the guest accommodations are behind the main building in a ten-room annex. Each has a private bath, and is furnished with antiques.

A full country breakfast is included in the room rate, and the dining room is open to the public for breakfast and lunch.
Season: Open year round.
Dining: Breakfast and lunch served to public.
Children: Welcome.
Pets: Not permitted.
Payment: No credit cards. Personal checks accepted.
Directions: Turn south on Highway 276 in center of Brevard. Go four blocks. Inn is on left.

The Inn at Brevard. *Brevard, North Carolina.*

Rates: Range from $38 to $45, double occupancy. Full breakfast included in room rate.

Bryson City

FOLKESTONE LODGE
Route 1, Box 310, West Deep Creek Road
Bryson City, North Carolina 28713
(704) 488-2730
Innkeepers: Bob and Irene Kranich

Folkestone's guests receive an enthusiastic welcome from Bob and Irene Kranich, a young couple who have transformed this old mountain farmhouse into a top-notch bed and breakfast. "We live here just like the guests," says Bob. "We're a bit bigger than some B. & B.s, but smaller than a real lodge."

With only five guest rooms, the inn is small enough to be personal, yet offers the "big city" convenience of private baths. The rooms are furnished with antiques. Flagstone floors, exposed brick, claw-footed tubs and wardrobes combine to give the inn a homey, old-fashioned feel.

Irene serves a full country breakfast which includes her specialty, hot fruit cobbler. Bob describes himself as "the maintenance man," and is also available to guide guests on overnight camping trips into the mountains.

The lodge is only a ten-minute walk from the Deep Creek entrance to the Great Smoky Mountains National Park. Whether one is searching for a relaxing retreat or an active vacation, the Kranichs are happy to oblige. Says Bob cheerfully, "Our guests set the mood."

Season: Open May through November.
Dining: No meals served to public.
Children: Welcome.
Pets: Not permitted.
Payment: Visa, MasterCard & personal check.
Directions: Follow green "Deep Creek Camp Ground" signs out of Bryson City. Lodge will be on left before campground.
Rates: $48, double occupancy. Full breakfast included in room rate.

FRYEMONT INN
P.O. Box 459
Bryson City, North Carolina 28713
(704) 488-2159
Innkeepers: George and Sue Brown

This rustic mountain inn was built in 1922 by Captain Amos Frye, a prominent local attorney who purchased land in the Smokies before the turn of the century at less than a dollar an acre.

Frye had his lumber crews choose the very best chestnut, oak and maple for the building. Many furnishings were handmade by mountain craftsmen. "It was certainly built with native materials," smiles innkeeper George Brown. "They used six inches of clay in the walls and attic for insulation."

The inn was closed for a time in the fifties and sixties, and is virtually unchanged from its early days, with the exception of the addition of private baths in each room. "We are trying hard to keep the inn like it was," says Brown.

Meals are served in the wood-beamed dining hall with its huge stone fireplace that accommodates ten-foot logs. The inn has a tennis court, shuffleboard and a large, secluded swimming pool that sits on a tree-covered hillside. "It was built in the forties, and we're told it was the first swimming pool built west of Asheville," says Brown.
Season: Open April through October.
Dining: Breakfast and dinner served to public.
Children: Welcome.
Pets: Not permitted.
Payment: Visa, MasterCard & personal check.
Directions: Take Bryson City exit off 19-A. Go .3 of a mile and turn right at sign.
Rates: Range from $36 to $42, double occupancy.

HEMLOCK INN
Bryson City, North Carolina 28713
(704) 488-2885
Innkeepers: John and Ella Jo Shell

To reach the Hemlock Inn one drives up a winding country road that leads to the top of a wooded mountain. The inn sits on 65 acres adjoining the Great Smoky Mountains National Park, and from this vantage point one has a wonderful view of the Alarka range in the distance.

"Our philosophy," says John Shell, "is to provide a place for people to get away from everyday life. The majority of our guests stay for several days, though we're delighted to have guests even if it's just for one night. Most of them come back and stay a week the next time."

The inn operates on a Modified American Plan (two meals included in room rate), and a bell is rung to summon guests to the dining room. Hearty, family-style meals are served at large, round tables equipped with lazy-susans, and a typical dinner includes two meats, four vegetables, homemade rolls and dessert. Only on Sunday is a noon meal served, but guests will be fixed a box lunch on request.

The Shells are unabashedly enthusiastic about the natural beauty that surrounds the inn. "We do everything we can to encourage people to get out and experience the outdoors," says John. "We're only a short distance from the best hiking trails in the world. Everybody isn't a hiker, but just strolling along a trail feeds the soul."

The inn offers illustrated talks by a retired Park naturalist to introduce guests to local flora and fauna. "When you learn what to look for, it opens up a whole new world," says Shell. Although there is no swimming pool, guests enjoy tubing in nearby Deep Creek.

There are 25 guest rooms, including three cottages, all with private baths and decorated in a relaxed country style. There are no phones or TVs. "Most guests don't miss them. They're too busy visiting with each other and enjoying the scenery."

Season: Open May through October.
Dining: Breakfast and dinner served to public by reservation only.
Children: Welcome.
Pets: Not permitted.
Payment: No credit cards. Personal checks accepted.
Directions: One mile off Highway 19, halfway between Bryson City and Cherokee.
Rates: Range from $80 to $90, double occupancy. Full breakfast and dinner included in room rate. (Modified American Plan)

RANDOLPH HOUSE
Fryemont Road, P.O. Box 816
Bryson City, North Carolina 28713
(704) 488-3472
Innkeepers: Bill and Ruth (Randolph) Adams

In 1895, Captain Amos Frye built a three-story frame house in the small mountain town of Bryson City. Captain Frye was a prominent lawyer, and his wife was the first female attorney in the state. The Fryes loved to entertain, a trait they passed on to their daughter who, after her marriage to John Randolph, opened the home to guests, calling it Peaceful Lodge.

Business was brisk and in 1923 the family built the Fryemont Inn beside the main house, substantially expanding the business. The Fryemont is now a separate establishment, but John Randolph's niece Ruth and her husband Bill moved to the mountains from Atlanta to continue the Randolph House's tradition of welcoming travelers.

The home has changed very little since the 19th century, and the Fryes' original furniture, including tall black-walnut beds, white wicker chairs and old woven rugs, still fill the place. There are six guest rooms; one on the first floor with a private bath, and five upstairs with several shared baths.

In 1978, the Randolph House began serving meals to the public (by reservation) because guests had spread the word about Ruth's cooking. "We never had a formal opening," says Ruth. "People just started calling and requesting reservations for dinner."

There are no printed menus; when you make a reservation you pick an entrée (Cornish hen, trout, prime rib, among others). "From that point," laughs Ruth, "you never know what you'll get." Diners might be treated to any number of vegetable dishes, and Ruth always bakes plenty of her hot yeast rolls as well as homemade desserts ranging from cobblers to chess pie. "Ruth isn't afraid to experiment," says Bill proudly. "She comes up with dishes that are really special."

Meals are served in the dining room as well as the parlor which is over 40 feet long. On warm nights, the French doors opening onto the terrace are flung wide, and guests enjoy their meals "out-of-doors."

Season: Open April through October.
Dining: Breakfast and dinner served to public by reservation.
Children: No children under 12, please.
Pets: Not permitted.

Payment: American Express, Visa, MasterCard & personal check.
Directions: Follow Rt. 19-A into Bryson City. Turn right (uphill) at inn sign before reaching first traffic light.
Rates: Range from $90 to $110, double occupancy. Full breakfast and dinner included in room rate.

Burnsville

NU-WRAY INN
P.O. Box 156
Burnsville, North Carolina 28714
(704) 682-2329
Innkeeper: Betty Wray Souders

In 1867, Betty Wray Souder's great-grandfather purchased an eight-room stagecoach stop, and although it has undergone some changes since those early days, it is still a family business. As a child, Betty liked to "work" behind the desk; in her teens she waited tables, and today she is the fourth generation of her family to manage the inn.

Although the original log cabin is buried in the heart of the building, numerous additions have pushed the inn outward and upward. The greatest changes came in 1917 when the third floor was added, along with plumbing and a heating system. "The inn had been dark brown until that time," says Betty. "When grandfather added the third floor and the columned front porch, he painted the whole building white. Everyone in town kept talking about the 'new' Wray Inn, and the name stuck."

There are 31 guest rooms, 25 with private baths. Antiques fill every nook and cranny, and a walk through the parlors is a stroll into the past. Family-style meals are served in the dining hall at long tables placed end to end.

The Nu-Wray has long been known for its country ham. At one time the hams were cured in the smoke house that still stands at the rear of the inn. "We can't use it anymore," says Betty wistfully. "We have to buy our hams because of government regulations. But if you open the door, even a crack, you can still smell the hickory smoke."
Season: Open year round.
Dining: Dining room open May 1 through December 1. Breakfast, dinner and Sunday lunch served to the public. Reservations

preferred.
Children: Welcome.
Pets: Not permitted, but arrangements for kenneling may be made in advance.
Payment: No credit cards. Personal checks accepted.
Directions: On the town square (Highway 19-23) in Burnsville.
Rates: Range from $25 to $37, double occupancy.

Candler

PISGAH VIEW RANCH
Rt. 1
Candler, North Carolina 28715
(704) 667-9100
Innkeeper: Ruby Cogburn

The 1,700-acre Pisgah View Ranch is part of a land grant awarded to Benjamin Davis in the 1790s. He settled in picturesque Hominy Valley in full view of mile-high Mt. Pisgah, built a sturdy log cabin and began to farm.

Today, his descendants still farm these same acres. The family homestead is now a turn of the century white frame farm house, but the cabin has been lovingly preserved. The family began to take in boarders around 1900, and although the Ranch has grown into a modern resort, guests still receive a hearty country welcome from the Cogburn family.

There are 50 guest rooms, each with private bath, in a variety of cottages. All three meals are included in the room rate. Guests enjoy swimming, tennis and horseback riding. In addition, some form of entertainment (bluegrass music, square dancing, etc.) is offered nightly.

Ruby's daughter, Phyllis, works in the office and a daughter-in-law, Mary, is in charge of the craft shop. The sense of history is very strong. Family portraits decorate the walls, and a quilt on display contains grey squares made from an ancestor's Confederate uniform.

"It's certainly a family business," laughs Phyllis. "We all hope that one of the next generation will want to carry on the tradition."
Season: Open May 1 through November 1.
Dining: All three meals served to public, by reservation.

Children: Welcome.
Pets: Discouraged.
Payment: No credit cards. Personal checks accepted.
Directions: Take Enka-Candler exit off I-40, go west on U.S. 19-23 for five miles to Candler. Turn left on NC-151. Follow signs eight miles.
Rates: Range from $66 to $100, double occupancy. All three meals included in room rate. (Full American Plan) ·

Cashiers

HIGH HAMPTON INN & COUNTRY CLUB
P.O. Box 338
Cashiers, North Carolina 28717
(704) 743-2411

High Hampton is a modern resort with all the amenities. For many years the estate was the summer home of the Hamptons of South Carolina. Wade Hampton III, Confederate general and U.S. Senator, spent much of his boyhood here.

The property, grown to include 2,200 acres, remained in the Hampton/Halsted family until the 1920s. A small inn was constructed in the twenties, but a fire in the thirties destroyed it as well as all the original buildings. The present inn dates from 1933.

The lodge is rustic, with huge stone chimneys and rooms featuring country-style furniture. The manicured grounds offer tennis, trap shooting, horseback riding, and three lakes for all sorts of water sports. The inn's management is particularly proud of their 18-hole, par 71 golf course designed by golf architect George W. Cobb. The 8th hole is considered one of America's great golf challenges.
Season: Open April 1 through November 1.
Dining: All three meals served daily to public.
Children: Welcome.
Pets: Not permitted at inn, but kennel is available.
Payment: American Express & personal check.
Directions: Turn south in Cashiers at the intersection of 64 and 107 and follow 107 for two miles to inn entrance.
Rates: Range from $90 to $114, double occupancy. All three meals included in room rate. (Full American Plan)

Chimney Rock

THE CORBETT HOUSE INN
Route 74
Chimney Rock, North Carolina 28720
(704) 625-4403
Innkeepers: Bob and Anne Corbett

The newly renovated Corbett House Inn (once the Old Logan Inn) stands beside U.S. 74 in the tiny town of Chimney Rock. The town itself has become oppressively "touristy" with shops selling bric-a-brac of all descriptions, so the Corbett Houses' tasteful exterior catches the eye, as do the handmade gifts displayed in a large first floor window.

Anne Corbett's gift shop, featuring *only* handmade items fills one corner of the ground floor. Her love of early American country styles is evident, not only in the shop but throughout the house. Adjoining the shop is a large sunny dining room, where the Corbetts hope eventually to open a tea room. The family quarters are in the back half of the house. The original old Hart range is still in place (and in use) in the kitchen.

The Corbetts purchased the building in 1982 and spent almost a full year restoring it. "We stripped five layers of paint off the hardwood floors," Anne says. The bed and breakfast inn opened in April 1983.

The seven guest rooms, located on the second floor, share two baths. Guests also have access to a TV/sitting room. Ann has hand-stenciled traditional designs around the rooms, and guests read a blessing stenciled on the stair risers as they ascend; "Health, Wealth, Peace and Happiness to All Who Enter This House."

Season: Open year round.
Dining: No meals served to public.
Children: Welcome.
Pets: Discouraged.
Payment: Visa, MasterCard & personal check.
Directions: On U.S. 74 in "downtown" Chimney Rock.
Rates: Range from $30 to $35, double occupancy. Continental breakfast included in room rate and dinner served to guests on request.

ESMERALDA INN
Box 57
Chimney Rock, North Carolina 28720
(704) 625-9105
Innkeepers: Pete and Pam Smith

The Esmeralda first opened its doors in 1892, though the present building dates from 1916. In that year the Broad River overflowed its banks and rampaged through the river gorge, leveling the inn to its foundations. Many of the original timbers were recovered and the inn was reconstructed.

The lobby is most unusual. Tree limbs still protrude from the unskinned log supports, and a second floor interior balcony is reached by a rough hewn staircase. The 13 guest rooms, six with shared baths, occupy the second and third floors. The decor throughout is classic country. For total privacy, there are several chalets available by the day or week.

Hollywood discovered the Esmeralda before the days of the talkies. Several silent movies were filmed on the site *(Esmeralda* and *In the Heart of the Blue Ridge)* and stars such as Clark Gable, Douglas Fairbanks and Mary Pickford vacationed here. Lew Wallace finished the screenplay for *Ben Hur* while staying in Room Nine.

Season: Open March 15 through November 15.
Dining: Dinner served to public, Tuesday through Saturday. Noon meal served on Sunday. Dining room closed on Monday.
Children: Welcome.
Pets: Not permitted.
Payment: Visa & MasterCard. Personal checks accepted for room deposit only.
Directions: On Highway 74 in Chimney Rock.
Rates: Range from $27 to $75, double occupancy. Continental breakfast served to guests.

Dillsboro ✓

THE JARRETT HOUSE
P.O. Box 219
Dillsboro, North Carolina 28725
(704) 586-9964
Innkeepers: Jim and Jean Hartbarger

The Jarrett House has been greeting guests continuously since 1884.
The tiny town of Dillsboro perches alongside the railroad tracks that
run from Asheville to Waynesville. The Jarrett House (originally
known as the Mount Beulah Hotel) was the lunch stop en route.
Passengers would hike the short distance up the hill, eat their fill
and continue on their journey.

Nine years ago Jim and Jean Hartbarger purchased the inn and
spent long hours refurbishing it. Says Jim, "We lived in three rooms,
and for the first three years we ploughed every nickle back into the
business."

Today, the Jarrett House is once again synonymous with country
cooking that leaves even the heartiest eater satisfied. "Our goal,"
Jim says, "is to provide good food and good service, at a decent
price."

The 18 guest rooms are furnished entirely with antiques, and all
have private baths. The inn celebrated its 100th birthday in 1984,
and has a personality all its own. The floors slope pleasantly and the
exposed water pipes add visual interest. There are three floors, and
guests enjoy relaxing in the row of rockers that grace the front porch
and both balconies. The Hartbargers like to remind guests of an old
Spanish proverb, "How beautiful it is to do nothing, and then to rest
afterward."

Season: Open April through October.
Dining: Three meals served daily to public.
Children: No children under 12, please.
Pets: Not permitted.
Payment: No credit cards. Personal checks accepted.
Directions: Located at junction of U.S. 441 and U.S. 19-A in Dillsboro.
Rates: $28, double occupancy.

The Jarrett House. *Dillsboro, North Carolina.*

Flat Rock

WOODFIELD INN
Box 98
Flat Rock, North Carolina 28731
(704) 693-6016
Innkeeper: David Levin

The Woodfield Inn (originally known as the Farmer Hotel) opened its doors in 1852 and has been receiving guests continuously since that date. In its early days, the inn served as a stagecoach stop on the old Buncombe Turnpike, a busy road that was once an Indian footpath.

Henry Tudor Farmer, who operated the inn from 1853 until his death in 1883, was well known in the south for designing the "Flat Rock rocker," a walnut rocking chair that didn't "creep" as one rocked in it. Farmer is also credited with developing the lemon-julep, a combination of bourbon, lemon juice, sugar, and spring water.

During the Civil War, a company of Confederate soldiers was garrisoned at the inn, and townsfolk brought their valuables and deposited them in the "secret room" on the second floor for safekeeping.

Despite its long history, the inn has had very few owners and has been lovingly cared for through the years. When the Levin family purchased the building in 1981 they undertook a meticulous restoration which took more than a year to complete. Professors from the University of Pennsylvania conducted a chemical analysis to determine the original colors used in the building, and these have been faithfully reproduced.

For their efforts, the Levins received a first place award as "Inn of the South" from the National Register of Historic Places. "In 1850, the total cost of building the inn was $950," says Levin with a smile. "It cost us ¾ million to return it to that condition."

There are 18 guest rooms, three with private baths, and all decorated with antiques. Most have fireplaces, and by modern standards are amazingly large. Meals are served in three high ceilinged dining rooms on the ground floor, and while the menu varies, the quality is consistently high. Breads and pastries are homemade, and many of the vegetables are grown on the inn's 25 acres.

Season: Open year round.

Dining: Lunch and dinner served to public daily.
Children: Welcome.
Pets: Not permitted.
Payment: American Express, Visa, MasterCard, & personal check.
Directions: On 25-South 2½ miles out of Hendersonville.
Rates: Range from $65 to $90, double occupancy. Continental breakfast included in room rate.

Franklin

BUTTONWOOD INN
190 Georgia Road
Franklin, North Carolina 28734
(704) 369-8985
Innkeeper: Liz Oehser

The Buttonwood is tucked into a grove of trees between the 5th and 7th greens of the Franklin Golf Course. Most of the guests are avid golfers and when they aren't playing, they sit under the trees and watch someone else play.

The Buttonwood is a bed and breakfast inn with four guest rooms, two with private baths, and two sharing a hall bath. The inn was built as a summer cottage in the 1920s, and turned into an inn in 1981. The decor is country casual with antiques scattered throughout the building.

Season: June 1 through October 31.
Dining: No meals served to public.
Children: By prior arrangement only.
Pets: Not permitted.
Payment: No credit cards. Personal checks accepted.
Directions: Follow U.S. 23/441 South out of Franklin. Inn is on right, adjacent to golf course.
Rates: Range from $35 to $55, double occupancy. Full breakfast included in room rate.

POOR RICHARD'S SUMMIT INN
East Rogers Street, P.O. Box 511
Franklin, North Carolina 28734
(704) 524-2006
Innkeeper: Minnie L. Hays

Five years ago, Richard and Minnie Hays purchased an old Victorian home and 2½ acres "atop the highest hill in Franklin," and they have created an inn so appealing that guests stop prospective guests in the lobby and deliver testimonials.

The house was built in 1898 by S.L. Rogers, a former director of the U.S. Bureau of Census. In 1928 a daughter converted the house into an inn, but the property faced an uncertain future in the 1970s until purchased by the Hays.

Today, the inn is in the latter stages of restoration and has been nominated for inclusion in the National Register. The view from the summit includes the Wayah Mountain range and the little Tennessee River.

Furnished entirely with turn of the century antiques, the rooms are cooled by wood-blade ceiling fans. There are 14 guest rooms, most with private baths. Around dinner time the nine dining rooms located on the ground floor of the inn become crowded with folks anxious to enjoy an enormous family-style meal. There is nothing "to do" at the inn except eat and relax. Minnie Hays says simply, "The Summit Inn is our home we share with friends."

Season: Open year round with limited operation during winter season. Phone for details.

Dining: Dinner served to public Monday through Saturday. Both lunch and dinner served on Sunday.

Children: Welcome.

Pets: Not permitted.

Payment: No credit cards. Personal checks accepted.

Directions: Take Business 411 into Franklin. Inn is on top of hill, on East Rogers Street.

Rates: Range from $35 to $40, double occupancy. Continental breakfast included in room rate.

Hendersonville

HAVENSHIRE INN
Route 4, Box 455, Cummings Road
Hendersonville, North Carolina 28739
(704) 692-4097
Innkeepers: Cindy Findley & Kay Coppock

The drive to the Havenshire is a beautiful way to begin a vacation. Winding country roads travel through field and forest, often following the French Broad River. Havenshire was built in 1882 and has served as a country retreat for a succession of owners. It was opened as a bed and breakfast inn by the present owners in 1981.

The house sits on 40 acres overlooking the French Broad River. There are six guest rooms, two with private baths, and two shared baths for the other four. The rooms open off a long airy hallway on the second floor. The ground floor, with its high ceilinged rooms, is elegantly furnished.

Bowman's Bluff, which is on the property, was named, so the legend goes, for Mary Bowman, a beautiful young woman who lived in the area during frontier times. She was a superb horsewoman and loved to ride at breakneck speed along the river bluffs. The legend tells of Mary's rejection by her lover. Broken hearted, she rode to the bluff and plunged into the river on horseback.

Season: Open April through October.
Dining: No meals served to public.
Children: Welcome.
Pets: Not permitted.
Payment: Visa, MasterCard & personal check.
Directions: Take U.S. 64 out of Hendersonville. Take the first left (Cummings Road) past the community of Horseshoe. Inn is approximately eight miles out of Hendersonville.
Rates: $60 to $65, double occupancy. Continental breakfast included in room rate.

THE WAVERLY
783 North Main Street
HOTEL McCURRY—755 North Main Street
Hendersonville, North Carolina 28739 (704) 692-6856
Innkeeper: J. Edwin McCurry

The Waverly and the Hotel McCurry sit side by side on tree shaded lots in the heart of Hendersonville. They have been operating continuously as guest houses since 1900. Mr. McCurry has run The Waverly for 25 years, and the Hotel for 13. Both houses have been nominated to the National Register.

There are a total of 45 rooms in both buildings with a wide range of accommodations. Nightly rooms are available, but the majority are rented on a weekly or monthly basis. "Hendersonville is becoming a town of retirees," says McCurry. "We provide a homelike atmosphere where they can feel comfortable. Until two years ago we didn't even have keys for the front door."

Most of McCurry's oldsters have stories to tell, such as the woman who, as a child of five at Fort Abraham Lincoln, watched Custer and his men ride off to the Little Big Horn in 1876. "Y'know," McCurry laughs, "she'd lived here for years before she told us that story. She didn't want anyone to know how old she was."

Season: Hotel McCurry: Open June through October. Waverly: Open year round.

Dining: No meals served to public.

Children: Welcome.

Pets: Not permitted.

Payment: No credit cards or personal checks. Cash or travelers checks only.

Directions: Located downtown on North Main Street.

Rates: Range from $25 to $40, double occupancy. Breakfast and dinner included in room rate.

Highlands

HIGHLANDS INN
Main Street, Box 1030
Highlands, North Carolina 28741
(704) 526-9380
Innkeepers: Glenn and Shan Arnette

The long, wood-frame structure of the Highlands Inn dominates Main Street as it has for over 100 years. "My wife and I wanted a home in the mountains," laughs Glenn Arnette. "Now we have a great big house with lots of nice house guests."

The inn was totally renovated in 1983, and the lobby features thick carpets, brass fixtures, and white-ruffled curtains. Music from an 1890's upright grand piano serenades guests in the dining room which glimmers with Waterford crystal. "We are mountain with a European flair," says Arnette.

The inn offers a variety of accommodations, most with private baths. Guests have the option of paying for lodgings only, or taking advantage of the inn's full American plan (room with three meals).

The Arnettes are enthusiastic about their mountain community. With an elevation of 4,100 feet, Glenn describes Highlands as "the top. All you can do is look over and *down* from here."

Season: Open mid-April through October. Limited off season accommodations available. Phone for details.
Dining: Three meals served daily to public.
Children: Welcome.
Pets: Not permitted.
Payment: American Express, Visa, MasterCard & personal check.
Directions: Located on Main Street in downtown Highlands.
Rates: $45, double occupancy.

The Old Edwards Inn. *Highlands, North Carolina.*

KING'S INN
P.O. Box 878
Highlands, North Carolina 28741
(704) 526-2161
Innkeepers: Charles and Norma Westerveld

Built as a private residence in 1883, the King's Inn has been operating as an inn for 90 years or more. Totally renovated in 1982, the inn is tastefully decorated with reproductions and antiques. Its airy first floor lobby opens onto broad porches.

"People have been coming here for generations," says Charles Westerveld, the inn's manager. "But Highlands is still a small mountain town. The city fathers have banned fast food establishments and so on. Highlands is a place to relax."

The inn has 33 guest rooms; 22 in the original building and 11 in cottages on the grounds. All rooms have private baths. "Our inn," says Westerveld, "has the old atmosphere, with the modern conveniences."

Season: Open May through October.
Dining: Three meals served daily to public.
Children: Welcome.
Pets: Not permitted.
Payment: Visa, MasterCard & personal check.
Directions: On route 28 at Spring Street in Highlands.
Rates: Range from $48 to $75, double occupancy.

THE OLD EDWARDS INN
Main Street
Highlands, North Carolina 28741
(704) 526-5036
Innkeeper: Rip Benton

In 1981 the Bentons purchased a bedraggled boarding house on the Main Street of Highlands. The original frame structure had been receiving guests since its construction in 1878. After seven months of hard work, the old inn and its 1930s brick addition have a new lease on life.

"We've restored it as authentically as possible...within reason," smiles owner, Rip Benton. "Some of the original walls were lath and paper; you could actually stick your hand right through them." In addition to replacing these walls with something more substantial, the pot-bellied stoves were removed, and the squirrel's nests cleaned out of the walls. "We found over 25 old coins, and hundreds of nuts," recalls Benton.

The inn has a country flavor, spiced with occasional pieces of stained glass and brass light fixtures. The Bentons went as far as New Orleans for the antiques that fill each room. Lovely handpainted stencils decorate the walls, the result of over 200 hours of labor by master stenciler Brenda Kellum.

The Central House restaurant, located in the 19th century portion of the inn, is a country-style dining room with a touch of elegance. The menu includes some mountain dishes, but the restaurant's well-deserved reputation for excellence is based primarily on their seafood entrées.

The inn has 21 guest rooms, most with balconies and all with private baths. "That's another improvement," says Benton with a smile, "there used to be only one bathroom on the entire third floor."

Season: Open May through October.

Dining: Lunch and dinner served to the public.

Children: Welcome.

Pets: Not permitted.

Payment: American Express, Visa, MasterCard & personal check.

Directions: Located on Main Street in downtown Highlands.

Rates: $55, double occupancy. Continental breakfast included in room rate.

Linville

ESEEOLA LODGE
Linville, North Carolina 28646
(704) 733-4311
Innkeeper: John Blackburn

The manicured grounds of the Eseeola Lodge lie in the tiny town of Linville, just below Grandfather Mountain. There has been an inn on this spot since the 1890s, but the present structure was built in the 1920s and 30s. Its lovely chestnut siding has led to its nomination to the National Register.

A long covered walkway made of rustic, bark-covered logs delivers guests to the front door, and the inn's wood-paneled interior is elegant yet welcoming. Each room has a private porch, brightened with well-tended window boxes. The inn operates under a modified American plan, with breakfast and dinner included in the room rate.

The inn's recreational offerings are varied and include golf, swimming, horseback riding, tennis, and trout fishing.

Season: Open late May through mid-September.

Dining: Breakfast and dinner served to public by reservation.

Children: Welcome.

Pets: Not permitted.

Payment: Visa & MasterCard.

Directions: On U.S. 221 in the town of Linville.

Rates: Range from $120 to $150, double occupancy. Breakfast and dinner included in room rate. (Modified American Plan)

Maggie Valley

SMOKY SHADOWS LODGE
Maggie Valley, North Carolina 28751
(704) 926-0001
Innkeepers: Bud, Ginger, Tracy, Chris,
Trevor & Amy Jo Shinn

As a child growing up in Miami in the 1950s, the highlight of Ginger Shinn's year was a vacation at Smoky Shadows. Now, years later, she is the proud owner of this piece of mountain property.

"Owning this lodge was my childhood fantasy," says Ginger, "and thanks to my family, it's come true." The lodge had changed hands several times over the years and was standing empty when the Shinns purchased it. "There are so many things that need to be done," Ginger says. "My goal is to recreate the homey feeling the lodge used to have."

The living room, with its exposed beams, is an old log grist mill, moved from its original location in the Cataloochee Valley. A large stone fireplace dominates one end of the room, and a roughhewn staircase on the opposite wall leads to the second floor. Built entirely of handhewn logs, the lodge contains such rarities as handcarved wooden door latches and wormy chestnut planking.

The 12 guest rooms, all with private baths, open off either side of the long hall connecting the great room and the dining area. The rooms are small but inviting, with handmade quilts on the beds and big fluffy towels in the baths.

The lodge sits at an elevation of 4,500 feet, and the view from the front porch is magnificent. A large maple tree shades one end of the building, and a rope swing hangs from its branches; with a strong push, one can soar over the embankment and above the treetops on the hillside below. The Shinns recently refurbished the swimming pool, and volley ball and shuffleboard are also available.

"I'm still learning about this business," Ginger smiles, "but I love it. I've always liked to entertain, and that's what I'm doing now—on a big scale."

Season: Open December through February and May through October.
Dining: Breakfast and dinner served to public by reservation.
Children: No children under five, please.
Pets: Not permitted.
Payment: Visa, MasterCard & personal check.
Directions: In Maggie Valley, follow signs to Ghost Town amusement park on Rt. 19. Follow road up hill on the left side of parking lot. Lodge is one mile up road. Watch for sign on right.
Rates: $45, double occupancy. Full breakfast included in room rate.

CATALOOCHEE RANCH
Rt. 1, Box 500
Maggie Valley, NC 28751
(704) 926-1401
Innkeepers: Tom and Alice Aumen

Cataloochee Ranch celebrated its 50th anniversary in 1984, as did its next door neighbor, the Great Smoky Mountains National Park. In the 1930s Alice Aumen's father had the foresight to realize that the growing number of guests to the area would need a place to stay. He purchased a large tract of land bordering the Park, and Cataloochee Ranch was born.

The Ranch consists of 1,000 acres of high mountain country. The main lodge building (elevation 5,000 feet) is a log barn with a fieldstone foundation, built in 1870. Renovated in 1939, it contains the dining area, as well as ten guest rooms, all with private baths. The rooms are decorated with antiques, quilts and handmade furniture.

Guests may choose to stay in one of the seven cabins that dot the grounds. All of them have private baths, and most have working fireplaces. Two of them are pioneer structures, built on the property more than a century ago.

A wide range of outdoor activities are available. "Our guests are very active types," says Alice Aumen. "Horseback riding is very popular, because we have some of the finest riding trails in the eastern U.S." Full and half day rides (with guides) are offered and back-country rides into the Park, lasting from one to ten days, can be arranged. Facilities for tennis, swimming and trout fishing are also on hand.

With an elevation of 5,000 feet, Cataloochee is the highest full facility guest ranch in the east. Even in summer the temperature rarely rises above 80°, and guests frequently enjoy a cozy fire on summer evenings.

"People used to ask my father why he started the Ranch," says Alice. "He always said, 'It's the only way I could live on top of a mountain and make a living at it.'"

Season: Open mid-May through mid-October. (Cataloochee Ski Area, a modern sister facility one mile up the mountain, is open during the winter months.)

Dining: Breakfast, lunch and dinner served to the public by reservation.

Children: No children under six, please.

Pets: Not permitted.

Payment: American Express, Visa, MasterCard & personal check.

Rates: Range from $76 to $125, double occupancy. Choice of two full meals included in room rate. (Modified American Plan)

Mars Hill

HISTORIC BAIRD HOUSE
121 South Main Road
Mars Hill, North Carolina 28754
(704) 689-5722 or 689-4542
Innkeepers: Jeanne T. Hoffman and Elizabeth Narron

The mountain town of Mars Hill has a population of less than 4,000, almost a third of whom are students at Mars Hill College, a four-year Baptist school. Many of the other residents are connected with the college in some capacity, and Jeanne Hoffman is no exception; her husband is Dean of the college.

The Hoffmans felt the B. & B. accommodations they had experienced while traveling in Europe would translate nicely to this small college town, and the Baird House is the result.

The Baird family built the substantial brick home just before the turn of the century, and the house became a center of community life, as Dr. John Baird was the only medical doctor in the area. For years Dr. John's daughter, "Aunt Lex" Baird, worked as a nurse, riding horseback into remote mountain areas to provide the only medical care available to many families. When she "retired" she began taking in college students as boarders.

There are six guest rooms, three with private baths. In addition, three of the rooms have working fireplaces. The home is furnished with period pieces, and guests receive a "North Carolina version of a continental breakfast," which includes sausage-cheese scones and apple fritters prepared especially for the Baird House by a local German bakery.

Season: Open year round.
Dining: No meals served to public.
Children: Welcome.
Pets: Not permitted.
Payment: No credit cards. Personal checks accepted.
Directions: Take Mars Hill "exit" off 19-23N, drive to first stop light. Take a left. Inn is several houses down on the left.
Rates: Range from $40 to $45, double occupancy. "North Carolina" continental breakfast included in room rate.

Pisgah Forest

PINES COUNTRY INN
Route 2, Hart Road, P.O. Box 7
Pisgah Forest, North Carolina 28768
(704) 877-3131
Innkeepers: Tom and Mary McEntire

The Pines sits on a hill overlooking the Little River Valley, an unspoiled expanse of fields and forests. Built in 1883 as a private home, the Pines has been an inn since 1905. The McEntires acquired it in 1971 and have lavished attention on the inn and the 12 acres that surround it.

The McEntires owned a furniture business in Florida before purchasing the Pines. Regarding their change of careers, Mary says simply, "It was meant to be." A born innkeeper, Mary attends to every detail herself. She does all the cooking, having learned from the Pines' previous cook who retired after 30 years at the inn. She also made the dining room tablecloths and not only keeps them spotless, but ironed.

There are 26 guest rooms, including several log cabins and cottages. Most have private baths and all are sparkling, cleaned by Mary or her daughter Ann, the only ones able to meet Mary's high standards.

Breakfast and dinner are included in the room rate, and guests certainly get their money's worth. "I had to order special ten-inch plates—regular ones weren't large enough," says Mary, describing the enormous family-style meals she serves. "We don't want to be a fancy inn," she adds. "We really want our guests to feel at home."

Season: Open May through October.
Dining: Dinner served to public six days a week, by reservation. On Sunday, only lunch is served, also by reservation.
Children: Welcome.
Pets: Not permitted.
Payment: No credit cards. Personal checks accepted.
Directions: Approximately eight miles from midtown Brevard. Once in area, phone inn for directions.

Pines Country Inn. *Pisgah Forest, North Carolina.*

Rates: $58, double occupancy. Breakfast and dinner included in room rate.

Robbinsville

BLUE BOAR LODGE
Joyce Kilmer Forest Road, Rt. 1, Box 46-A
Robbinsville, North Carolina 28771
(704) 479-8126
Innkeepers: Roy and Kathy Wilson

This unpretentious mountain lodge is nestled in a hollow of the Nantahala National Forest. Built originally as a private hunting lodge, it was purchased by the Wilsons in 1983.

Recreation and relaxation are the primary reasons for a stay at the Blue Boar. There are mountain paths to explore, and Lake Santeetlah, with its 108 miles of shoreline, is less than a mile away. It offers excellent opportunities for swimming, boating, fishing and canoeing. Bring your own boat, or check with the Wilsons about boat rentals (at very reasonable rates).

Hunting and fishing guides are available for anyone uncertain of his skills as a woodsman. And for those who don't wish to invest in a license, private fishing is available in the lodge's own trout pond. (There is no limit and you pay by the pound.) During the late fall and early winter, the lodge accommodates hunters for bear and boar season.

There are only eight guest rooms. They have rustic furnishings and private baths. Breakfast and dinner are served family-style from an eight foot table equipped with a lazy-susan. Kathy, who does all the cooking, will pack picnic lunches by request.
Season: Open April 1 through mid-October. Additional season for hunters, October 15 through January 1.
Dining: No meals served to public.
Children: Welcome.
Pets: Not permitted.
Payment: Visa & MasterCard. Personal checks discouraged.
Directions: Located on Joyce Kilmer road, ten miles from Robbinsville. Follow Blue Boar signs out of Robbinsville on Route 129.

Rates: $50, double occupancy. Breakfast and dinner included in room rate.

SNOWBIRD MOUNTAIN LODGE
Joyce Kilmer Road, Rt. 1
Robbinsville, North Carolina 28771
(704) 479-3433
Innkeepers: Bob and Connie Rhudy

The view from the balcony of the Snowbird is one of the most breathtaking in all of North Carolina. One sees range after range of mountains, as well as the blue waters of Lake Santeetlah, far below.

The lodge, constructed of stone and native wood, is rustic and comfortable. Built in the 1940s shortly after the creation of the Great Smoky Mountains National Park, this area was, at that time, one of the most isolated in the eastern U.S. Even today, visitors can sense the isolation imposed on past generations by these rugged mountains.

Guest rooms are paneled in a variety of native woods, with custom-made furniture to match. All rooms have private baths. The lodge operates on a Full American Plan, meaning all three meals are included in the room rate.

Relaxing and communing with nature are the major recreations, and, says Connie, "Some guests return two or three times a year, just to experience the various seasons here."

Season: Open late April through early November.
Dining: All three meals served to public, by reservation.
Children: No children under 12, please.
Pets: Not permitted.
Payment: American Express, Visa & MasterCard. Personal checks preferred.
Directions: Located ten miles N.W. of Robbinsville on Joyce Kilmer Road. Follow signs from Robbinsville.
Rates: Range from $84 to $89, double occupancy. All three meals included in room rate.

Saluda

THE ORCHARD INN
P.O. Box 725
Saluda, North Carolina 28773
(704) 749-5471
Innkeepers: Ken and Ann Hough

This inn brings city sophistication to a mountain setting. The Houghs moved to the mountains from South Carolina where they had restored several homes in Charleston's historic district.

The inn was built by the Southern Railway Company at the turn of the century as a summer retreat for their employees, but had deteriorated sadly by the time it was purchased by the Houghs. Completely renovated, the inn is beautifully decorated with furniture brought from Charleston. The high ceilinged living room has heavy carpets, sofas stacked with pillows and baskets of all descriptions.

The eight guest rooms, all with private baths, are upstairs. A sculpture gallery and a bakery occupy the basement. The Wildflour bakery provides the inn (and other area establishments) with fresh, whole-grain breads. Ken is in charge of the inn's kitchen and the gourmet meals that result.

"We've been pretty well tied here for three years. We've only managed separate vacations," smiles Ann. Explaining the couples' commitment to quality she says simply, "Guests here are guests in our home."

Season: Open year round.
Dining: Dinner served to public, by reservation. (Jackets required for gentlemen.)
Children: No children, please.
Pets: Not permitted.
Directions: Located on Route 176 two miles from I-26 and one mile from Saluda.
Payment: No credit cards. Personal checks accepted.
Rates: $68, double occupancy. Full breakfast included in room rate.

THE WOODS HOUSE
Drawer E
Saluda, North Carolina 28773
(704) 749-9562
Innkeepers: Roy and Dorothy Eargle

On the side of a steep slope in the town of Saluda sits the Woods House, a large frame building with a broad, breezy, wrap-around porch. It was built in 1892 to serve as a lodge and was owned by the Woods family in the early 1900s, hence its name.

The house is packed with antiques, compliments of Roy and Dorothy Eargle's other business, a successful antique dealership in Alexandria, Virginia. "We're slowly easing out of antiques," explains Roy. "We intend to 'retire' to Saluda, so we're building up the inn business now."

Only two of the buildings' three floors are open at present, but the Eargles plan to expand their present total of six guest rooms. Guests have a choice of accommodations with private or shared baths, as well as a cottage on the grounds. Almost every room in the house boasts some sort of antique trunk, one of the couples' favorite collectibles. Several of their huge, oak-ribbed trunks were once borrowed by the White House as decorative containers for masses of Christmas presents.

Running two businesses seems to agree with this energetic couple. "I really enjoy the inn," Roy says. "I am continuously learning from our guests. All of them are interesting."

Season: Open May 1 through November 30.
Dining: No meals served to public.
Children: No children, please.
Pets: Not permitted.
Payment: No credit cards. Personal checks accepted only if approved in advance.
Directions: One block off Main Street, at the corner of Church and Henderson.
Rates: Range from $35 to $50, double occupancy. Continental breakfast, full breakfast and dinner available to guests for additional fee.

Tryon

MILL FARM INN
P.O. Box 1251
Tryon, North Carolina 28782
(704) 859-6992
Innkeepers: Chip and Penny Kessler

The Mill Farm Inn, on the outskirts of Tryon, is an attractive stone building built as an inn in 1939. It was converted into a private home in the early fifties and remained so until purchased by Chip and Penny Kessler in 1981.

The inn operates as a bed and breakfast, but is somewhat different from the usual establishment because the Kesslers do not live on the premises. Although they generally meet guests as they check in, they then become invisible hosts. In the morning the continental breakfast (juice, cereal, coffee, fruit breads and muffins) is automatically warmed with timers; guests simply help themselves.

The eight bedrooms, all with private baths, are tastefully decorated with furnishings in a traditional style, spiced with occasional antiques. Guests have access to a fully equipped kitchen, pleasant living room, dining area and sitting porches. The inn stands on 3½ beautifully landscaped acres, and the Pacelot river flows past the rear of the building.

The Mill Farm is perfect for travelers who would like a home-like atmosphere, yet are uncomfortable with a more traditional B. & B.

Season: Open March through December.
Dining: No meals served to public.
Children: Welcome.
Pets: Not permitted.
Payment: No credit cards. Personal checks accepted.
Directions: On Route 108, 2½ miles off I-26 and 1½ miles from downtown Tryon.
Rates: $48, double occupancy. Continental breakfast included in room rate.

Pine Crest Inn. *Tryon, North Carolina.*

PINE CREST INN
P.O. Box 1030
Tryon, North Carolina 28782
(704) 859-9135
Innkeepers: Bob and Helene Johnson

The Pine Crest is a "country" inn in the middle of the tiny town of Tryon. The inn's manicured grounds and tall trees give a feeling of isolation though guests are surrounded with city conveniences.

Built in 1906 as a tuberculosis sanitarium, the main building houses the dining facilities and a limited number of guest rooms. Most of the accommodations are in cabins and cottages scattered throughout the grounds.

There are 31 guest rooms, all with private baths, most with fireplaces, and many with sitting rooms. Several of the cottages have picturesque names such as Twain, Woodcutter and Swayback. The latter, so named because of its sloping roofline, housed F. Scott Fitzgerald during his visits.

Bob and Helene Johnson purchased Pine Crest in 1983 after seeing an ad in the *Wall Street Journal*. "This place just jumped out from a list of inns all up and down the east coast," Bob explains.

The inn is one of Tryon's favorite dining spots, and is open daily to the public for all three meals. A cozy atmosphere is enhanced by a low wood-beamed ceiling where white-jacketed waiters lavish diners with attention.

Season: Open year round.
Dining: Three meals served daily to public. (Gentlemen required to wear coats for dinner.)
Children: Welcome.
Pets: Not permitted.
Payment: No credit cards. Personal checks accepted.
Directions: In downtown Tryon, go south on Trade Street. Take a left on New Market Road. Go .2 of a mile and turn left onto Pine Crest Lane.
Rates: Range from $60 to $100, double occupancy.

STONE HEDGE INN
P.O. Box 366
Tryon, North Carolina 28782
(704) 859-9114
Innkeeper: John Weiner

The Stone Hedge sits on a tree-shaded knoll at the base of Tryon
Mountain. The inn is at 1,100 feet while the mountain towers upward
an additional 2,500 feet.

In this quiet country setting, John Weiner, a graduate of the pres-
tigious Culinary Institute of America, discovered a stone house that
had stood empty for several years. "My wife and I had looked for a
place to open as a restaurant for quite some time. We settled on
Tryon because we have relatives nearby, and we thought continental
cuisine would go over well here."

Weiner is quick to point out that the restaurant is the cornerstone
of the inn's operation. "We only have four guest rooms, three upstairs
in the main building, as well as one cottage on the grounds, but
more rooms are planned." The rooms all have private baths and are
decorated with a mixture of antiques and contemporary pieces.
Guests are free to enjoy the swimming pool located on a terraced
piece of land at the front of the inn.

The restaurant can seat up to 60, and uniformed waiters provide
guests with attentive service. The specialty of the house is beef Wellington. "We don't serve a lot of southern-style food," says Weiner. "I'd
describe us as continental and quasi-nouvelle. I love to create new
dishes, but there just isn't enough time."

Season: Closed three weeks in winter—dates vary.
Dining: Dinner is served to the public, Wednesday through Saturday.
Only lunch is served on Sundays.
Children: No children under six, please.
Pets: Not permitted.
Payment: Visa, MasterCard & personal check.
Directions: Take Exit 36 off I-26 onto NC-108 heading toward Tryon.
Go three miles. Turn right on Howard Gap Road. The inn is 1½
miles, on the right.
Rates: Range from $50 to $68, double occupancy. Full breakfast in-
cluded in room rate.

Waynesville

HALLCREST INN
299 Halltop Road
Waynesville, North Carolina 28786
(704) 456-6457
Innkeepers: Russell and Margaret Burson

From the front porch of the Hallcrest Inn guests have a marvelous view of Waynesville below, as well as Lickstone Bald, part of the Balsam range, in the distance. Russell, a retired Methodist minister, and Margaret, a teacher, have run the inn for four years, but, says Margaret, "We are not professional innkeepers. I still occasionally get the biscuits in the oven on pre-heat."

The old frame farmhouse sits at the end of a winding gravel road. It is 110 years old, and has plenty of atmosphere, including an old tin roof, pine paneling and dormer windows.

The inn caters to groups during the off season months; November through mid-December, and April through mid-May. "We want to provide a facility for retreats, where groups can get away from it all. But they don't have to be church groups," Russell explains. "We are happy to have ski groups, and so on."

There are eight guest rooms in the farm house and four in a recent addition. The new rooms are in modern motel-style. All rooms have private baths. A full breakfast and family-style dinner are served in the dining room which is equipped with large, lazy-susan tables.

An old dinner bell hangs just outside the kitchen door, and is rung at eight o'clock for wake-up, and eight-thirty for breakfast. The Bursons also ring the bell whenever guests leave, "to wish them a safe journey home."

Season: Open June through October. Available for groups during off season. Closed January and February.

Dining: Family-style dinner and Sunday lunch served to public by reservation.

Children: Welcome.

Pets: Not permitted, but arrangements for kenneling may be made in advance.

Payment: No credit cards. Personal checks accepted.

Directions: From 19A/23 take Waynesville/Brevard exit onto U.S. 276.
Follow 276, 1.3 miles. Take left on Mauney Cove Rd. and go 1.2
miles. Turn left up hill on gravel road. Inn is .6 of a mile.
Rates: $52, double occupancy. Full breakfast and dinner included in
room rate.

HEATH LODGE
900 Dolan Road
Waynesville, North Carolina 28786
(704) 456-3333
Innkeepers: David and Bonnie Probst

The Probsts, a suburban Chicago couple, came south searching for a
"new and more rewarding lifestyle." They purchased Heath Lodge in
1980. Bonnie is in charge of the kitchen, and David, formerly an
architect, attends to the other details of innkeeping.

The lodge sits in a grove of trees on eight acres, and the site feels
secluded even though it is actually in town. The inn was built in the
forties from native stone and wood. The dining room and office
occupy one building, and guest rooms are dispersed in several
smaller buildings. All rooms have private baths.

Bonnie's family-style meals resulted in so many requests for
recipes the Probsts compiled a cook book, *Heath Lodge Favorites*,
which guests may want to purchase after sampling such dishes as
corn meal dumplings or scalloped cabbage.

Season: Open late May through late October.
Dining: Breakfast, dinner and Sunday lunch served to the public by
reservation.
Children: Welcome.
Pets: Discouraged.
Payment: No credit cards. Personal checks accepted.
Directions: Follow 276 south toward Waynesville. Turn right onto
Dellwood Drive just after Kentucky Fried Chicken. Follow signs.
Rates: Range from $50 to $60, double occupancy. Full breakfast and
family-style dinner included in room rate.

THE PIEDMONT INN AND MOTOR LODGE
630 Eagles Nest Road, P.O. Box 419
Waynesville, North Carolina 28786
(704) 456-8636
Innkeeper: Jane McKay

A comfortable country inn built in the 1880s, the Piedmont sits on
the slopes of Eagle's Nest Mountain. The inn's elevation is around
3,000 feet; the mountain rises upward an additional 2,000 feet. The
original white frame inn, surrounded by tall oaks and maples, boasts
broad, airy hallways and a pleasant dining area decorated with fresh
flowers grown on the grounds.

   A small motor lodge offers more ⌐ ⌐⌐⌐.y accommodations,
including color TVs in each r⌐⌐ ⌐⌐, spring-fed swimming pool
and a tree-shaded clay t⌐ ⌐⌐⌐ are open to guests at both the inn
and lodge.

   The lodge is op. ⌐⌐. round, but the inn closes during the winter
months. It is heateu by two wood-burning stoves located on the first
floor, and though they keep guests warm during the surprisingly cool
summer evenings, they were deemed inadequate for winter needs.
Season: Inn open May through October. Lodge open year round.
Dining: No meals served to public.
Children: Welcome.
Pets: Permitted at lodge. Not permitted at inn.
Payment: Visa, MasterCard & personal check.
Directions: Take Hazelwood exit off 19A/23. Follow Eagle's Nest Road
one mile.
Rates: Range from $27.50 to $37, double occupancy. Continental
breakfast included in room rate during summer season.

THE SWAG
Rt. 2, Box 280-A
Waynesville, North Carolina, 28786
(704) 926-0430
Innkeepers: Dan and Deener Matthews

The Matthews first saw the 250 acres they now own in an aerial
photograph. They were looking for a secluded place to build a second
home and a "sometimes" retreat for the congregations Dan serves as
an Episcopal minister. They completed their dream retreat in 1970,

The Swag. *Waynesville, North Carolina.*

and in 1982 they decided to turn it into an inn. The Swag is the result.

Located high on a mountain (elevation 5,000 feet) adjoining the Great Smoky Mountains National Park, this inn is the perfect place to get away from it all. To reach the Swag, guests drive 6½ miles off the main highway, much of it over unpaved roads. The inn's driveway is 2½ miles long, and the Matthews' nearest neighbor is over a mile away as the crow flies.

The Swag was built by combining five old log structures, including a primitive Baptist church. There are 11 guest rooms, most with a fireplace or wood-burning stove, and all with private baths.

The atmosphere is pure Appalachia. Colorful patchwork quilts decorate walls as well as beds. Early American furniture, arts, and crafts greet guests at every turn. Old wooden rockers line the front porch which overlooks the valley far below. On a clear day Mount Mitchell, more than 50 miles away, can be seen. "We opened an inn," says son Danny, indicating the magnificent view, "because we wanted to share all this."

Season: Open late May through October.

Dining: Dinner served to public if reservation made 24 hours in advance.

Children: Welcome.

Pets: Not permitted.

Payment: Visa, MasterCard & personal check.

Directions: Off U.S. 276 north of Waynesville, turn west onto Hemphill Road, continue four miles to Swag driveway.

Rates: Range from $82 to $98, double occupancy. Full breakfast and dinner included in room rate.

Cohutta Lodge. *Chatsworth, Georgia.*

GEORGIA

Chatsworth

COHUTTA LODGE
5000 Cochise Trail
Chatsworth, Georgia 30705
(404) 695-9601
Innkeepers: Floyd and Julie Franklin

As one drives east out of the small town of Chatsworth, the imposing outline of Fort Mountain looms on the horizon. A ten-mile drive up a winding road leads to Cohutta Lodge perched on the mountain top. Situated on 300 acres at an elevation of 2,800 feet, the lodge offers a panoramic view of the Chattahoochee National Forest with peak after peak receding into the distance.

"The lodge is only ten years old, but it looks 50 because of the constant wind at this elevation," explains Julie Franklin. She and husband Floyd, formerly Atlanta residents, moved to the mountain in 1979. "Most folks envy our being able to live on the mountain year 'round," says Julie.

Despite its remote setting, Cohutta offers guests a wide range of amenities, including tennis courts and a heated indoor pool that is filled with well water. "You'd better explain what we mean by heated," Julie says with a grin. "The water comes out of the ground

THE SOUTHERN MOUNTAIN STATES
(Area of map shown below)

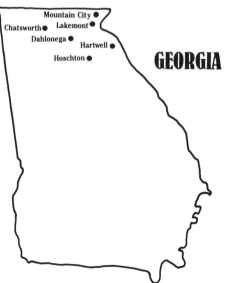

Mountain City ●
Chatsworth ●   Lakemont ●
Dahlonega ●
Hartwell ●
Hoschton ●

GEORGIA

at 52°, and we heat it to 82°; folks shouldn't expect a sauna." Other activities available to guests are horseback riding, hiking, fishing and, in winter, tobogganing on a slope carved out of the woods specifically for that purpose.

There are 60 guest rooms, 21 in the main lodge, 36 in a nearby annex, and three efficiencies. All have private baths. Furnishings are contemporary, with a few country touches such as ruffled Priscilla curtains and a large stone fireplace in the dining room.

Season: Open year round.
Dining: Three meals served daily to public.
Children: Welcome.
Pets: Not permitted.
Payment: American Express, Visa, MasterCard & personal check.
Directions: Ten miles east of Chatsworth on Rt. 52.
Rates: Range from $35 to $49, double occupancy.

Dahlonega

SMITH HOUSE
202 S. Chestatee
Dahlonega, Georgia 30533
(404) 864-3566
Innkeepers: Fred and Shirley Welch

The food at the Smith House is so good folks have been known to wait *five* hours for one of their family-style meals. "Until we completed an addition to the dining room, we sometimes had as many as 600 people waiting out in the yard," says owner Fred Welch, Jr.

The Smith House is a Georgia tradition that dates back to 1922 when the Smith family opened their late 19th century frame home to boarders. The Welch family took over in 1946, and Fred Jr. is the second generation to keep the tradition alive.

"The thing we're proudest of is our *fresh* vegetables," says Welch. "We make a special effort to serve them fresh all year round. During the summer we may use 15 bushels of green beans a week." To keep the kitchen supplied, Welch hires senior citizens to string beans, and clean and chop other vegetables.

Diners are seated on a first-come-first-served basis and although the menu changes daily, there are always three meats and nine to eleven vegetables available.

The frame house, as well as the original carriage house, contain 18 guest rooms, all with private baths. Each room is decorated differently, but all have a country feel.

Dahlonega is called "America's First Gold Rush City," since gold was discovered there in 1828, nearly 20 years before the California gold rush. A U.S. mint was built in the town in 1838 and minted over $6,000,000 in gold pieces before it was shut down.

The town square is the epitome of small town America (although many of the shops now cater primarily to tourists) and the old courthouse has been converted into a museum of gold history.

Season: Open year round.

Dining: Three meals served to public Tuesday through Sunday, from May through November. Phone for off-season schedule.

Children: Welcome.

Pets: Not permitted.

Payment: Visa & MasterCard. NO personal checks.

Directions: One block south of the town square on highway 60.

Rates: $37.44, double occupancy.

WORLEY HOMESTEAD, BED AND BREAKFAST INN
410 West Main Street
Dahlonega, Georgia 30533
(404) 864-7002
Innkeepers: Mick and Mitzi Francis

The Worley Homestead sits two blocks off Dahlonega's town square, a sturdy white two-story frame house built in 1845 and home to the Worley family from 1872 to 1932. In recent years the home had begun to show its age as sagging beams and water damage took their toll. In 1983, the Francis family bought the property and restored it, a project especially important to Mitzi because the Homestead is her ancestral home. (Mitzi's great grandfather was Captain William Jasper Worley, a veteran of the Battle of Atlanta and a community leader in Dahlonega until his death in 1913.)

Today, after an intensive eight-month restoration, the Homestead has been refurbished, both inside and out. The seven guest rooms, each with private bath, are named for members of the Worley family, and all rooms are furnished in antiques of the period. A two-bedroom, one-bath cottage on the grounds is also furnished with antiques and includes a fully equipped kitchen. To complete the 19th century feeling, hostesses for the Homestead wear period dress.

The large brick chimneys on either end of the house are particularly interesting. The bricks were made locally and traces of gold dust, embedded in the clay, glitter when struck by the sun.

Season: Open year round.

Dining: No meals served to public.

Children: Welcome.

Pets: Not permitted.

Payment: American Express, Visa, MasterCard & personal check.

Directions: On highway 52, two blocks west of the town square, directly across the street from the gold steeple of North Georgia College.

Rates: Range from $45, double occupancy, but vary with the season. Full breakfast included in room rate.

Hartwell

HARTWELL INN
504 W. Howell Street
Hartwell, Georgia 30643
(404) 376-3967
Innkeeper: Mary Jo Swanson

Mary Jo Swanson opened her Hartwell home to guests in 1980. "I stayed at an inn in northern California and loved the homey feel it gave me. When we moved to Georgia I decided this house would make a wonderful inn."

Situated on an acre of land in the tiny town of Hartwell, the inn is one of the town's oldest buildings. The foundation was laid in 1914 and it took three years to complete the building. The 16-room house has 12-foot ceilings and a wide entry way with stairs leading to the second floor where the guest rooms are located.

Upstairs, the broad hallway functions as a sitting room, enticing guests to sit and read or visit. "I do everything in the world to encourage guests to enjoy the entire house," says Mary Jo.

The five guest rooms share two baths, one on the first and one on the second floor. The furnishings are a mixture of antiques and

Hartwell Inn. *Hartwell, Georgia.*

contemporary pieces and the effect is homey rather than elegant. Mary Jo's love of bright colors (particularly "Georgia red") is evident throughout the house.

Recently a guest asked if rates could be reduced since he didn't want breakfast, and Mary Jo, who does all the cooking herself, replied with a smile, "The rates won't change because breakfast is a *gift* I give my guests. No amount of money would make me get up and cook every morning."

Season: Open year round.
Dining: No meals served to public.
Children: Welcome.
Pets: Not permitted.
Payment: No credit cards. Personal checks accepted.
Directions: Take Lavonia exit off I-85 and go south. Inn is at intersection of U.S. 29 and Route 77 in Hartwell.
Rates: $45, double occupancy. Full breakfast included in room rate.

Hoschton

HILLCREST GROVE
Peachtree Road
Hoschton, Georgia 30548
(404) 654-3425
Innkeeper: Dennis Pitters

When Dennis Pitters first saw Hillcrest Grove it was standing empty, many of its windows missing and the porches overgrown with ivy. "Amazingly, the interior woodwork and hardware were intact," says Pitters who teaches hotel/restaurant management at Georgia State. "I'd been looking for two years for a house suited to be a bed and breakfast, and I knew this was it."

Built around the turn of the century as the residence for the 2,000-acre Hill family plantation, the house sits in a grove of pecan trees which shade its broad front porch. "The house was amazingly solid despite being neglected in recent years," says Pitters, indicating the brick work which looks brand new. "It took four years to build the house and they took great pains with it, even to the point of letting it 'rest' for a year with weights on the roof to prevent future settling."

The house has 22 rooms and 12-foot ceilings, upstairs as well as down. The interior woodwork is mahogany and the hardware is brass. A massive mahogany arch and an open-well staircase greet guests in the entry hall.

The four guest rooms are upstairs and share two baths. The upstairs hall, broad and airy, doubles as a sitting room, and guests enjoy relaxing on the second floor balcony. The guest rooms have fireplaces and are furnished in antiques.

"We keep things very low key," says Pitters, "and we accept guests *only* by reservation." Those fortunate enough to enjoy a stay at Hillcrest Grove are served a continental breakfast featuring coffeecake made from the farm's pecans.

Season: Open year round.
Dining: No meals served to public.
Children: By prior arrangement only.
Pets: Not permitted.
Payment: No credit cards. Personal checks accepted.
Directions: Take Braselton exit (number 49) off I-85. Go two miles south on Route 53. House will be on your right.
Rates: Range from $35 to $45, double occupancy. Continental breakfast included in room rate.

Lakemont

THE LAKE RABUN HOTEL
Box 101-A
Lakemont, Georgia 30552
(404) 782-4946
Innkeepers: Dick and Barbara Gray

The Lake Rabun Hotel sits on 4½ wooded acres. Built on the lake shore in 1922, the hotel "was about the only thing out here at that time," says Dick Gray.

Few things have changed since those days. The rugged stone fireplace still fills one corner of the lobby, and the board and batten walls create a rustic, peaceful atmosphere. One of the most interesting features is the rhododendron furniture made especially for the inn 60 years ago.

There are 16 guest rooms, four downstairs and 12 upstairs. They are furnished simply but comfortably, and the majority have shared baths.

Situated in the midst of the Chattahoochee National Forest, the inn is just steps away from a lakeside marina, Rabun Beach Recreation Area is four miles down the road, and some of the state's finest river rafting is nearby.

The inn's atmosphere is informal; hiking boots are perfectly acceptable attire. There are no phones, no TVs, and the inn's water is supplied by several springs. "This is the second wettest county in the country," says Barbara. Besides numerous springs, there are a great many waterfalls which provide refreshing destinations for hikers.

Season: Open April 1 through October 30.

Dining: No meals served to public.

Children: Welcome.

Pets: Not permitted.

Payment: No credit cards. Personal checks accepted.

Directions: Follow U.S. 441-23 six miles south of Clayton. Turn right at the Wiley Junction Store and follow road to left. Inn is four miles farther on the right.

Rates: $25, double occupancy. Continental breakfast included in room rate.

Mountain City

YORK HOUSE
P.O. Box 126
Mountain City, Georgia 30562
(404) 746-2068
Innkeepers: Philip and Ingrid Sarris

In the late 19th century "Little Mama" York and her family settled on 40 acres deeded to her from her grandfather, one of the area's earliest settlers. A log cabin which had been an overseer's house before the Civil War stood on the site, and the family gradually added to it, creating a comfortable frame farm house typical of the period.

When the first railroad was being surveyed through the mountains, "Little Mama," so-called because of her diminutive stature, boarded the surveyors and, later, the summer guests who found their way into these isolated hills.

The property passed out of the York family in 1979, but a granddaughter still lives nearby, and the present proprietors have continued the inn's tradition of down-home hospitality.

"This is a very special, very serene place," says innkeeper Ingrid Sarris. "Even with a full house the peaceful quality isn't disturbed."

The original log building still stands in the heart of the home. Handhewn beams and the blackened fireplace of the slave quarters are still visible in the basement, but several additions over the years have resulted in a two-story frame building with white railed porches on both levels. Enormous Norwegian pines, planted before the Civil War, shade the front of the inn.

The 15 guest rooms, all with private baths, are furnished with antiques and each has its own charm. A continental breakfast is included in the room rate and is delivered to the room on a silver tray so that guests may enjoy a leisurely meal in bed.

Season: Open year round.

Dining: No meals served to the public.

Children: Well behaved children welcome.

Pets: Not permitted.

Payment: Visa, MasterCard & personal check.

Directions: Just off U.S. 23-441 in Mountain City.

Rates: Range from $38 to $41, double occupancy. Continental breakfast included in room rate.

INDEX TO INNS
by State and Town

INNS of the SOUTHERN MOUNTAINS

WHAT A TERRIFIC GIFT IDEA!

Which of your friends and relatives deserve invitations to the charms of the INNS OF THE SOUTHERN MOUNTAINS?

Send us their names and addresses, along with your gift cards, and we'll do the rest. The cost is but $10.45 per book including shipping and handling. (Virginia residents, please also add state tax of 36¢ for each book.)

If you order five books or more shipped to one address, we will pay all shipping and handling costs. Send check or money order to EPM Publications, Box 490, McLean, VA 22101.

TO HELP YOU PLAN AND ENJOY YOUR TRAVEL AND SPECIAL INTERESTS

EPM
PUBLICATIONS, INC.
1003 Turkey Run RD.
McLean, VA 22101
703/442-7810

ONE-DAY TRIPS THROUGH HISTORY   **$9.95**
Describes 200 historic sites within 150 miles of the nation's capital where our forebears lived, dramatic events occurred and America's roots took hold. Sites are arranged chronologically starting with pre-history.

ONE-DAY TRIPS TO BEAUTY AND BOUNTY   **$8.95**
Would you believe there are more than 150 garden getaways in and around Washington, D.C.? Something beautiful and refreshing for every season and taste, including special longer trips to 10 of the most magnificent East Coast gardens.

WASHINGTON ONE-DAY TRIPS   **$7.95**
101 fascinating excursions within a day's drive of the capital beltway—out and back before bedtime. The trips are arranged by seasons and accompanied by calendars of special events, map and notes on facilities for the handicapped.

Also:

Florida One-Day Trips (from Orlando). What to do after you've done Disney. **$4.95**

Call It Delmarvalous. How to talk, cook and "feel to hum" on the Delaware, Maryland and Virginia peninsula. **$7.95**

Old Alexandria. Copiously illustrated walking guide, to George Washington's hometown. **$5.95**

Footnote Washington. Tracking the engaging, humorous and surprising bypaths of capital history by one of the city's most popular broadcasters. **$7.95**

Mr. Lincoln's City. An illustrated guide to the Civil War sites of Washington, as readable as it is informative. **$12.95**

See next page for a convenient order blank.

BESTSELLING QUILT DESIGN BOOKS

JINNY BEYER
Patchwork Patterns
The revolutionary paper-folding system that cracks complicated mechanical draft-ing methods, enabling craftspeople to recreate geometric patterns in any size. 800 illus. **Pa, $15.95**
Quilter's Album of Blocks & Borders
The companion book to *Patchwork Patterns* compiles, names, documents, cate-gorizes and stunningly illustrates more than 700 patterns for easy drafting and identification. **Hc, $18.95**
Medallion Quilts
The art and technique of creating the finest of the 18th century designs, now all the rage again. Historic and contemporary examples, 40 in color. **Hc, $29.95**

JOYCE SCHLOTZHAUER
The Curved Two-Patch System
Magical new designs dispel the mystique about curves in patchwork and applique. **Pa, $16.95**
Curves Unlimited
With 107 block designs and 55 borders, this ultimate workbook shows how to mod-ify traditional hard-edged patterns. **Pa, $24.95**

Order Blank for all EPM books described here. Mail with check to:

EPM Publications, Inc.
Box 490, McLean, VA 22101

Title	Quantity	Price	Amount	Shipping
				Free if all to
Inns of the Southern Mountains	5	$8.95	$44.75	same address
Inns of the Southern Mountains	1–4	$8.95		$1.50 per book
		Subtotal		
	Virginia residents, add 4% tax			
Name _____	Shipping			
Street _____				
City _____ State ___ Zip ___	TOTAL			

Remember to enclose names, addresses and enclosure cards for gift purchases.
Please note that prices are subject to change. Thank you.

ABOUT THE AUTHOR

Patricia L. Hudson grew up in the mountains of east Tennessee and now resides in Knoxville. A Phi Beta Kappa history major, she also holds an M.S. in Information Science. She served three years as a reference librarian on the faculty of the University of Tennessee before resigning in 1983 to write full time. Her articles frequently reflect her fascination with the people and traditions of Appalachia and have appeared in such publications as *Americana, Country* and *American Heritage.*

As a reference librarian working on collection development in history, anthropology and travel, she covered the southern mountains area. Always looking for interesting places to stay and things to see and do, she quickly discovered a lack of sufficient resource material and a scattering of what information there was. She began compiling her own lists, and INNS OF THE SOUTHERN MOUNTAINS is the result.

She and photographer Sam Stapleton were married shortly after they completed their work on this book. They are now renovating a turn-of-the-century house, filling it with antiques and mountain crafts they acquired during their travels.